lo

T0011747

*Fast Talk*

# French

Guaranteed to get you talking

# Contents

## ≡ Special Features

# Before You Go

*Many visitors to France get around without speaking a word of French, but just a few phrases go a long way in making friends, inviting service with a smile, and ensuring a rich and rewarding travel experience – you could discover a cosy vineyard off the tourist track, experience a sublime meal, or grab that great shopping bargain.*

## PRONUNCIATION TIPS

The sounds of French can almost all be found in English, and if you read our coloured pronunciation guides as if they were English you'll be understood.

★ The few sounds that do differ from English include the throaty r (a bit like a growl) and ew (said as the 'ee' in 'see' with rounded lips). Note also that zh is pronounced as the 's' in 'pleasure'.

★ French has nasal vowels (pronounced as if you're trying to force the sound 'through the nose'). English is similar to some extent – eg when you say 'sing', the 'i' is nasalised

by the 'ng'. We've used nasal consonant sounds (m, n, ng) after the nasal vowel so you can produce the sound with confidence.

★ Syllables in French are, for the most part, equally stressed – as English speakers tend to stress the first syllable, try adding a light stress on the final syllable of French words to compensate.

## MUST-KNOW GRAMMAR

The structure of French holds no major surprises for English speakers since the two languages are quite closely related.

★ French has a formal and informal word for 'you' (*vous* voo and *tu* tew respectively). When talking to someone familiar or younger than you, use the *tu* form. Phrases in this book use the form that is appropriate to the situation. Where both forms can be used, they are indicated by pol and inf respectively.

★ French has masculine and feminine forms of words, eg *beau/belle* bo/bel (beautiful), indicated in this book by m and f respectively.

★ Verbs have a different ending for each person, like the English 'I do' vs 'he/she do**es**'. You'll still be understood if you use the dictionary form of a verb in all contexts.

## SOUNDS FAMILIAR?

Many French words are part of the English vocabulary – thanks to the Norman invasion of England in the 11th century, some estimate that three-fifths of everyday English vocabulary arrived via French. You'll recognise *café*, *déjà vu*, *rendez-vous*, *cliché* …

# Fast Talk French

Don't worry if you've never learnt French (*français* fron·say) before – it's all about confidence. You don't need to memorise endless grammatical details or long lists of vocabulary – you just need to start speaking. You have nothing to lose and everything to gain when the locals hear you making an effort. And remember that body language and a sense of humour have a role to play in every culture.

*"you just need to start speaking"*

Even if you use the very basics, such as greetings and civilities, your travel experience will be the better for it. Once you start, you'll be amazed how many prompts you'll get to help you build on those first words. You'll hear people speaking, pick up sounds and expressions from the locals, catch a word or two that you know from TV already, see something on a billboard – all these things help to build your understanding.

# 5. Phrases to Learn Before You Go

### 1. What are the opening hours?
**Quelles sont les heures d'ouverture?**
kel zon lay zer doo·vair·tewr

French business hours are governed by a maze of regulations, so it's a good idea to check before you make plans.

---

### 2. I'd like the set menu, please.
**Je voudrais le menu, s'il vous plait.**
zher voo·dray ler mer·new  seel voo play

The best-value dining in France is the two- or three-course meal at a fixed price. Most restaurants have one on the chalkboard.

---

### 3. Which wine would you recommend?
**Quel vin vous conseillez?** kel vun voo kon·say·yay

Who better to ask for advice on wine than the French?

---

### 4. Can I address you with 'tu'?
**Est-ce que je peux vous tutoyer?**
es·ker zher per voo tew·twa·yay

Before you start addressing someone with the informal 'you' form, it's polite to ask permission first.

---

### 5. Do you have plans for tonight?
**Vous avez prévu quelque chose ce soir?**
voo za·vay pray·vew kel·ker shoz ser swar

To arrange to meet up without sounding pushy, ask friends if they're available rather than inviting them directly.

---

6

# 10. Phrases to Sound Like a Local

| Cool! | **Génial!** | zhay·nyal |

| No worries. | **Pas de soucis.** | pa der soo·see |

| Sure. | **D'accord.** | da·kor |

| No way! | **Pas question!** | pa kay·styon |

| Just joking! | **Je plaisante!** | zher play·zont |

| Too bad. | **Tant pis.** | tom pee |

| What a shame. | **Quel dommage.** | kel do·mazh |

| What's up? | **Qu'est-ce qu'il y a?** | kes keel ya |

| Well done! | **Bien joué!** | byun zhoo·ay |

| Not bad. | **Pas mal.** | pa mal |

# 10. Phrases to Start a Sentence

BEFORE YOU GO

| | |
|---|---|
| **When is (the tour)?** | C'est quand (l'excursion)?<br>say kon (leks·kewr·syon) |
| **Where is (the station)?** | Où est (la gare)?<br>oo·ay (la gar) |
| **Where can I (buy a ticket)?** | Où peut-on (acheter un billet)?<br>oo per·ton (ash·tay um bee·yay) |
| **Do you have (a map)?** | Avez-vous (une carte)?<br>a·vay·voo (ewn kart) |
| **Is there (a toilet)?** | Y a-t-il (des toilettes)?<br>ya·teel (day twa·let) |
| **I'd like (a coffee).** | Je voudrais (un café).<br>zher voo·dray (ung ka·fay) |
| **I'd like to (return this).** | Je voudrais (rapporter ceci).<br>zher voo·dray (ra·por·tay ser·see) |
| **Can I (enter)?** | Puis-je (entrer)?<br>pweezh (on·tray) |
| **Do I have to (book a seat)?** | Faut-il (réserver une place)?<br>fo·teel (ray·zair·vay ewn plas) |
| **Can you (write down the price)?** | Pouvez-vous (écrire le prix)?<br>poo·vay voo (ay·kreer ler pree) |

# Chatting & Basics

## ≡ Fast Phrases

| | |
|---|---|
| **Hello./Goodbye.** | Bonjour./Au revoir.<br>bon·zhoor/o rer·vwar |
| **Please./Thank you.** | S'il vous plaît./Merci.<br>seel voo play/mair·see |
| **Do you speak English?** | Parlez-vous anglais?<br>par·lay·voo ong·glay |

## Essentials

| | |
|---|---|
| **Yes.** | Oui.<br>wee |
| **No.** | Non.<br>non |
| **Please.** | S'il vous plaît.<br>seel voo play |
| **Thank you (very much).** | Merci (beaucoup).<br>mair·see (bo·koo) |
| **You're welcome.** | Je vous en prie.<br>zher voo zon·pree |
| **Excuse me.** | Excusez-moi.<br>ek·skew·zay·mwa |
| **Sorry.** | Pardon.<br>par·don |

9

## Language Difficulties

| | |
|---|---|
| **Do you speak English?** | Parlez-vous anglais? par·lay·voo ong·glay |
| **Does anyone speak English?** | Y a-t-il quelqu'un qui parle anglais? ya·teel kel·kung kee par long·glay |
| **Do you understand?** | Comprenez-vous? kom·prer·nay·voo |
| **I understand.** | Je comprends. zher kom·pron |
| **I don't understand.** | Je ne comprends pas. zher ner kom·pron pa |
| **I speak a little.** | Je parle un peu. zher parl um per |
| **What does ... mean?** | Que veut dire ...? ker ver deer ... |
| **How do you pronounce this?** | Comment le prononcez-vous? ko·mon ler pro·non·say voo |
| **How do you write ...?** | Comment est-ce qu'on écrit ...? ko·mon es kon ay·kree ... |
| **Could you please repeat that?** | Pourriez-vous répéter, s'il vous plaît? poo·ree·yay voo ray·pay·tay seel voo play |
| **Could you please write it down?** | Pourriez-vous l'écrire, s'il vous plaît? poo·ree·yay voo lay·kreer seel voo play |

| Could you please speak more slowly? | Pourriez-vous parler plus lentement, s'il vous plaît?<br>poo·ree·yay voo par·lay plew lon·ter·mon seel voo play |
| --- | --- |
|  Slowly, please! | Lentement, s'il vous plaît!<br>lon·ter·mon seel voo play |

## Greetings

| Hello. | Bonjour.<br>bon·zhoor |
| --- | --- |
| Hi. | Salut.<br>sa·lew |
| Good morning/afternoon. | Bonjour.<br>bon·zhoor |
| Good evening/night. | Bonsoir.<br>bon·swar |
| See you later. | À bientôt.<br>a byun·to |
| Goodbye. | Au revoir.<br>o rer·vwar |
| How are you? | Comment allez-vous? pol<br>ko·mon ta·lay·voo<br>Ça va? inf<br>sa va |

**CHATTING & BASICS**

**Fast Talk** Greetings

A kiss on each cheek remains a common greeting in France, though between men (and when meeting a man or a woman for the first time) a handshake is more usual.

11

| Fine, thanks. And you? | Bien, merci.<br>Et vous/toi? **pol/inf**<br>byun mair·see<br>ay voo/twa |
| --- | --- |

## Titles

| Mr | Monsieur (M)<br>mer·syer |
| --- | --- |
| Ms/Mrs | Madame (Mme)<br>ma·dam |
| Miss | Mademoiselle (Mlle)<br>mad·mwa·zel |

## Introductions

| What's your name? | Comment vous appelez-vous? **pol**<br>ko·mon voo za·play·voo<br>Comment tu t'appelles? **inf**<br>ko·mon tew ta·pel |
| --- | --- |
| My name is ... | Je m'appelle ...<br>zher ma·pel ... |
| I'm pleased to meet you. | Enchanté(e). **m/f**<br>on·shon·tay |
| It's been great meeting you. | Ravi d'avoir fait ta connaissance. **inf**<br>ra·vee da·vwar fay ta ko·nay·sons |
| I'd like to introduce you to ... | Je vous présente ...<br>zher voo pray·zont ... |
| This is ... | Voici ...<br>vwa·see ... |

## PHRASE BUILDER

| This is my ... | Voici mon/<br>ma ... m/f | vwa·see mon/<br>ma ... |
|---|---|---|
| child | enfant | on·fon |
| colleague | collègue | ko·leg |
| friend | ami(e) m/f | a·mee |
| husband | mari m | ma·ree |
| partner | partenaire | par·ter·nair |
| wife | femme f | fam |

| | |
|---|---|
| What's your ...? | Quel est votre ... ? pol<br>kel ay vo·trer ...<br>Quel est ton ...? inf<br>kel ay ton ... |

## PHRASE BUILDER

| Here's my ... | Voici mon ... | vwa·see mon ... |
|---|---|---|
| address | adresse | a·dres |
| email | e-mail | ay·mel |
| mobile<br>number | numéro de<br>portable | new·may·ro der<br>por·ta·bler |
| phone<br>number | numéro de<br>téléphone | new·may·ro der<br>tay·lay·fon |

## Personal Details

| | |
|---|---|
| Where are you from? | Vous venez d'où? pol<br>voo ver·nay doo<br>Tu viens d'où? inf<br>tew vyun doo |

**PHRASE BUILDER**

| I'm from ... | Je viens ... | zher vyun ... |
|---|---|---|
| **Australia** | d'Australie | dos·tra·lee |
| **Canada** | du Canada | dew ka·na·da |
| **England** | d'Angleterre | dong·gle·tair |
| **New Zealand** | de la Nouvelle-Zélande | der la noo·vel·zay·lond |
| **the USA** | des USA | day zew·es·a |

| | |
|---|---|
| **Are you married?** | Est-ce que vous êtes marié(e)? m/f pol<br>es·ker voo zet mar·yay<br>Est-ce que tu es marié(e)? m/f inf<br>es·ker tew ay mar·yay |
| **I'm single.** | Je suis célibataire.<br>zher swee say·lee·ba·tair |
| **I'm married.** | Je suis marié(e). m/f<br>zher swee mar·yay |
| **I'm separated.** | Je suis séparé(e). m/f<br>zher swee say·pa·ray |

## Age

| | |
|---|---|
| **How old are you?** | Quel âge avez-vous? pol<br>kel azh a·vay·voo<br>Quel âge as-tu? inf<br>kel azh a·tew |
| **I'm ... years old.** | J'ai ... ans.<br>zhay ... on |
| **How old is your son/ daughter?** | Quel âge a votre fils/fille?<br>kel azh a vo·trer fees/fee·yer |
| **He/She is ... years old.** | Il/Elle a ... ans.<br>eel/el a ... on |

## Occupations & Study

| | |
|---|---|
| **What's your occupation?** | Vous faites quoi comme métier? pol<br>voo fet kwa kom may·tyay<br>Tu fais quoi comme métier? inf<br>tew fay kwa kom may·tyay |
| **I'm an office worker.** | Je suis un(e) employé(e)<br>de bureau. m/f<br>zher swee zun/zewn om·plwa·yay<br>der bew·ro |
| **I work in (education).** | Je travaille dans (l'enseignement).<br>zher tra·vai don (lon·sen·yer·mon) |

---

**PHRASE BUILDER**

| **I'm (a) ...** | Je suis<br>(un/une) ... m/f | zher swee<br>zun/zewn ... |
|---|---|---|
| retired | retraité(e) m/f | rer·tray·tay |
| self-<br>employed | indépendant(e) m/f | un·day·pon·don(t) |
| student | étudiant(e) m/f | ay·tew·dyon(t) |
| unemployed | chômeur m<br>chômeuse f | sho·mer<br>sho·merz |

---

| | |
|---|---|
| **What are you studying?** | Que faites-vous comme études? pol<br>ker fet·voo kom ay·tewd<br>Que fais-tu comme études? inf<br>ker fay·tew kom ay·tewd |
| **I'm studying engineering.** | Je fais des études<br>d'ingénieur.<br>zher fay day zay·tewd<br>dun·zhay·nyer |
| **I'm studying French.** | Je fais des études de français.<br>zher fay day zay·tewd der fron·say |

## Interests

| | |
|---|---|
| **What do you do in your spare time?** | Que fais-tu pendant tes loisirs? <br> ker fay·tew pon·don tay lwa·zeer |
| **Do you like (art)?** | Aimes-tu (l'art)? <br> em·tew (lar) |
| **Do you like (sport)?** | Aimes-tu (le sport)? <br> em·tew (ler spor) |
| **I like (music).** | J'aime (la musique). <br> zhem (la mew·zeek) |
| **I like (movies).** | J'aime (les films). <br> zhem (lay feelm) |
| **I don't like (cooking).** | Je n'aime pas (cuisiner). <br> zher nem pa (kwee·zee·nay) |
| **I don't like (hiking).** | Je n'aime pas (la randonnée). <br> zher nem pa (la ron·do·nay) |

## Feelings

| | |
|---|---|
| **Are you (cold)?** | Avez-vous (froid)? pol <br> a·vay voo (frwa) <br> As-tu (froid)? inf <br> a·tew (frwa) |
| **I'm (hot).** | J'ai (chaud). <br> zhay (sho) |
| **I'm not (hungry).** | Je n'ai pas (faim). <br> zher nay pa (fum) |
| **I'm not (thirsty).** | Je n'ai pas (soif). <br> zher nay pa (swaf) |

| Are you ...? | Êtes-vous ...? pol | |
|---|---|---|
| | et voo ... | |
| | Es-tu ...? inf | |
| | ay·tew ... | |
| I'm ... | Je suis ... | |
| | zher swee ... | |

### PHRASE BUILDER

| I'm not ... | Je ne suis pas ... | zher ner swee pa ... |
|---|---|---|
| happy | heureux m | er·reu |
| | heureuse f | er·reuz |
| in a hurry | pressé(e) m/f | pray·say |
| sad | triste | treest |
| tired | fatigué(e) m/f | fa·tee·gay |
| well | bien | byun |

## Numbers

| 0 | zéro | zay·ro |
|---|---|---|
| 1 | un | un |
| 2 | deux | der |
| 3 | trois | trwa |
| 4 | quatre | ka·trer |
| 5 | cinq | sungk |
| 6 | six | sees |
| 7 | sept | set |
| 8 | huit | weet |
| 9 | neuf | nerf |
| 10 | dix | dees |
| 11 | onze | onz |

| 12 | douze | dooz |
|---|---|---|
| 13 | treize | trez |
| 14 | quatorze | ka·torz |
| 15 | quinze | kunz |
| 16 | seize | sez |
| 17 | dix-sept | dee·set |
| 18 | dix-huit | dee·zweet |
| 19 | dix-neuf | deez·nerf |
| 20 | vingt | vung |
| 21 | vingt et un | vung tay un |
| 22 | vingt-deux | vung·der |
| 30 | trente | tront |
| 40 | quarante | ka·ront |
| 50 | cinquante | sung·kont |
| 60 | soixante | swa·sont |
| 70 | soixante-dix | swa·son·dees |
| 80 | quatre-vingts | ka·trer·vung |
| 90 | quatre-vingt-dix | ka·trer·vung·dees |
| 100 | cent | son |
| 1000 | mille | meel |
| 1,000,000 | un million | um meel·yon |

## Fast Talk   Telling the Time

The 24-hour clock is commonly used when telling the time in French. After the half hour, use the next hour minus (*moins* mwun) the minutes until that hour arrives, eg '20 to seven' is *Il est sept heures moins vingt* ee lay set er mwun vung.

## Time

| What time is it? | Quelle heure est-il?<br>kel er ay·teel |
|---|---|
| It's one o'clock. | Il est une heure.<br>ee·lay ewn er |
| It's (10) o'clock. | Il est (dix) heures.<br>ee·lay (deez) er |
| Quarter past (one). | Il est (une) heure et quart.<br>ee·lay (ewn) er ay kar |
| Half past (one). | Il est (une) heure et demie.<br>ee·lay (ewn) er ay der·mee |
| Quarter to (one). | Il est (une) heure moins le quart.<br>ee·lay (ewn) er mwun ler kar |
| At what time? | À quelle heure?<br>a kel er |
| At ... | À ...<br>a ... |
| in the morning | du matin<br>dew ma·tun |
| in the afternoon | de l'après-midi<br>der la·pray·mee·dee |
| in the evening | du soir<br>dew swar |

## Days

| Monday | lundi m | lun·dee |
|---|---|---|
| Tuesday | mardi m | mar·dee |
| Wednesday | mercredi m | mair·krer·dee |
| Thursday | jeudi m | zher·dee |
| Friday | vendredi m | von·drer·dee |

| | | |
|---|---|---|
| Saturday | samedi m | sam·dee |
| Sunday | dimanche m | dee·monsh |

## Months

| | | |
|---|---|---|
| January | janvier m | zhon·vyay |
| February | février m | fayv·ryay |
| March | mars m | mars |
| April | avril m | a·vreel |
| May | mai m | may |
| June | juin m | zhwun |
| July | juillet m | zhwee·yay |
| August | août m | oot |
| September | septembre m | sep·tom·brer |
| October | octobre m | ok·to·brer |
| November | novembre m | no·vom·brer |
| December | décembre m | day·som·brer |

### Fast Talk — Starting Off

When starting to speak another language, your biggest hurdle is saying aloud what may seem to be just a bunch of sounds. The best way to do this is to memorise a few key words, like 'hello', 'thank you' and 'how much?', plus at least one phrase that's not essential, eg 'how are you', 'see you later' or 'it's very cold/hot' (people love to talk about the weather!). This will enable you to make contact with the locals, and when you get a reply and a smile, it'll also boost your confidence.

## Dates

| | |
|---|---|
| **What date?** | Quelle date?<br>kel dat |
| **What's today's date?** | C'est quel jour aujourd'hui?<br>say kel zhoor o·zhoor·dwee |
| **It's (18 October).** | C'est le (dix-huit octobre).<br>say ler (dee·zwee tok·to·brer) |
| **yesterday morning** | hier matin<br>ee·yair ma·tun |
| **tomorrow morning** | demain matin<br>der·mun ma·tun |
| **yesterday afternoon** | hier après-midi<br>ee·yair a·pray·mee·dee |
| **tomorrow afternoon** | demain après-midi<br>der·mun a·pray·mee·dee |
| **yesterday evening** | hier soir<br>ee·yair swar |
| **tomorrow evening** | demain soir<br>der·mun swar |
| **last week** | la semaine dernière<br>la ser·men dair·nyair |
| **next week** | la semaine prochaine<br>la ser·men pro·shen |
| **last month** | le mois dernier<br>ler mwa dair·nyay |
| **next month** | le mois prochain<br>ler mwa pro·shen |
| **last year** | l'année dernière<br>la·nay dair·nyair |
| **next year** | l'année prochaine<br>la·nay pro·shen |

## Weather

| | |
|---|---|
| **What's the weather like?** | Quel temps fait-il?<br>kel tom fay·teel |
| **What's the weather forecast?** | Quelles sont les prévisions météo?<br>kel son lay pray·vee·zyon may·tay·yo |
| **It's (very) cold.** | Il fait (très) froid.<br>eel fay (tray) frwa |
| **It's hot.** | Il fait chaud.<br>eel fay sho |
| **It's raining.** | Il pleut.<br>eel pler |
| **It's snowing.** | Il neige.<br>eel nezh |
| **It's sunny.** | Il fait beau.<br>eel fay bo |
| **It's windy.** | Il fait du vent.<br>eel fay dew von |

## Directions

| | |
|---|---|
| **Where's (a bank)?** | Où est-ce qu'il y a (une banque)?<br>oo es·keel ya (ewn bongk) |
| **What's the address?** | Quelle est l'adresse?<br>kel ay la·dres |
| **Could you please write it down?** | Pourriez-vous l'écrire, s'il vous plaît?<br>poo·ree·yay voo lay·kreer seel voo play |

## Fast Talk  Negatives

To make a negative statement, French uses two words – *ne* ner and *pas* pa, both meaning 'not' – around the verb: *je ne sais pas* zher ner say pa (lit: I not know not). With another negative word in the sentence, *pas* is omitted: *je n'ai rien à déclarer* zher nay ryun a day·kla·ray (lit: I not-have nothing to declare).

| | |
|---|---|
| **Can you show me (on the map)?** | Pouvez-vous m'indiquer (sur la carte)? poo·vay·voo mun·dee·kay (sewr la kart) |
| **How far is it?** | C'est loin? say lwun |
| **Turn at the corner.** | Tournez au coin. toor·nay o kwun |
| **Turn at the traffic lights.** | Tournez aux feux. toor·nay o fer |
| **Turn left.** | Tournez à gauche. toor·nay a gosh |
| **Turn right.** | Tournez à droite. toor·nay a drwat |
| **behind ...** | derrière ... dair·yair ... |
| **in front of ...** | devant ... der·von ... |
| **next to ...** | à côté de ... a ko·tay der ... |
| **opposite ...** | en face de ... on fas der ... |
| **straight ahead** | tout droit too drwa |

# Airport & Transport

## ≡ Fast Phrases

| | |
|---|---|
| **When's the next (bus)?** | Le prochain (bus) passe à quelle heure? ler pro·shun (bews) pas a kel er |
| **Does this (train) stop at ...?** | Est-ce que ce (train) s'arrête à ...? es·ker se (trun) sa·ret a ... |
| **One ticket to ..., please.** | Un billet pour ..., s'il vous plaît. um bee·yay poor ... seel voo play |

## At the Airport

| | |
|---|---|
| **I'm here on business.** | Je suis ici pour le travail. zher swee zee·see poor ler tra·vai |
| **I'm here on holiday.** | Je suis ici pour les vacances. zher swee zee·see poor lay va·kons |
| **I'm here for (three) days.** | Je suis ici pour (trois) jours. zher swee zee·see poor (trwa) zhoor |

| | | |
|---|---|---|
| **I'm here for (two) weeks.** | Je suis ici pour (deux) semaines. | |
| | zher swee zee·see poor (der) ser·men | |
| **I'm in transit.** | Je suis ici de passage. | |
| | zher swee zee·see der pa·sazh | |
| **I'm going to (Paris).** | Je vais à (Paris). | |
| | zher vay a (pa·ree) | |
| **I have nothing to declare.** | Je n'ai rien à déclarer. | |
| | zher nay ryun a day·kla·ray | |
| **I have something to declare.** | J'ai quelque chose à déclarer. | |
| | zhay kel·ker·shoz a day·kla·ray | |

## Getting Around

### PHRASE BUILDER

| **At what time does the ... leave?** | À quelle heure part ...? | a kel er par ... |
|---|---|---|
| boat | le bateau | ler ba·to |
| bus | le bus | ler bews |
| plane | l'avion | la·vyon |
| train | le train | ler trun |

| **When's the first bus?** | Le premier bus passe à quelle heure? |
|---|---|
| | ler prer·myay bews pas a kel er |
| **When's the last bus?** | Le dernier bus passe à quelle heure? |
| | ler dair·nyay bews pas a kel er |
| **When's the next bus?** | Le prochain bus passe à quelle heure? |
| | ler pro·shun bews pas a kel er |

25

| How long does the trip take? | Le trajet dure combien de temps?<br>ler tra·zhay dewr kom·byun der tom |
| Is it a direct route? | Est-ce que c-est direct?<br>es·ker say dee·rekt |
| That's my seat. | C'est ma place.<br>say ma plas |
| Is this seat taken? | Est-ce que cette place est occupée?<br>es·ker set plas ay to·kew·pay |
| ✂ Is it taken? | C'est occupée?<br>say to·kew·pay |

## Buying Tickets

| Where can I buy a ticket? | Où peut-on acheter un billet?<br>oo per·ton ash·tay um bee·yay |
| Do I need to book? | Est-ce qu'il faut réserver une place?<br>es·keel fo ray·zer·vay ewn plas |

---

**Fast Talk**  **Reading French**

In written French, an *l'* in front of a word beginning with a vowel or a silent *h* replaces a *le* or a *la* (the) and is pronounced as if the word starts with an *l*, eg *l'orange* lo·ronzh (orange). Also, if one word ends with a consonant and the next word starts with a vowel or an *h*, run the sounds together as if they were one word – eg *vous avez* voo za·vay (you have). Otherwise don't pronounce a consonant at the end of a word, eg *faux* fo (false) – the exception is final *c*, eg *sec* sek (dry).

26

| What time do I have to check in? | Il faut se présenter à l'enregistrement à quelle heure? eel fo ser pray·zon·tay a lon·rer·zhee·strer·mon a kel er |
|---|---|

**PHRASE BUILDER**

| One ... ticket (to Paris), please. | Un billet ... (pour Paris), s'il vous plaît. | um bee·yay ... (poor pa·ree) seel voo play |
|---|---|---|
| 1st-class | de première classe | der prem·yair klas |
| 2nd-class | de seconde classe | der se·gond klas |
| child's | au tarif enfant | o ta·reef on·fon |
| one-way | simple | sum·pler |
| return | aller et retour | a·lay ay rer·toor |
| student's | au tarif étudiant | o ta·reef ay·tew·dyon |

| I'd like an aisle seat. | Je voudrais une place côté couloir. zher voo·dray ewn plas ko·tay koo·lwar |
|---|---|
| I'd like a window seat. | Je voudrais une place côté fenêtre. zher voo·dray ewn plas ko·tay fe·ne·trer |
| I'd like a (non)smoking seat. | Je voudrais une place (non-)fumeur. zher voo·dray ewn plas (non·)few·mer |

## Luggage

| | |
|---|---|
| **My luggage has been damaged.** | Mes bagages ont été endommagés.<br>may ba·gazh on tay·tay on·do·ma·zhay |
| **My luggage has been stolen.** | Mes bagages ont été volés.<br>may ba·gazh on tay·tay vo·lay |
| **My luggage has been lost.** | Mes bagages ont été perdus.<br>may ba·gazh on tay·tay per·dew |
| **I'd like a luggage locker.** | Je voudrais une consigne automatique.<br>zher voo·dray ewn kon·see·nyer o·to·ma·teek |
| **Can I have some coins/ tokens?** | Je peux avoir des pièces/ jetons?<br>zher per a·vwar day pyes/ zher·ton |

## Bus & Train

| | |
|---|---|
| **Where's the bus stop?** | Où est l'arrêt d'autobus?<br>oo ay la·ray do·to·bews |
| **Which bus goes to ...?** | Quel bus va à ...?<br>kel bews va a ... |
| **Is this the bus to ...?** | Est-ce que c'est le bus pour ...?<br>es·ker say ler bews poor ... |
| **What station is this?** | C'est quelle gare?<br>say kel gar |
| **What's the next station?** | Quelle est la prochaine gare?<br>kel ay la pro·shen gar |

| | |
|---|---|
| **Does this train stop at ...?** | Est-ce que ce train s'arrête à ...? |
| | es·ker se trun sa·ret a ... |
| **Do I need to change trains?** | Est-ce qu'il faut changer de train? |
| | es·keel fo shon·zhay der trun |
| **How many stops to ...?** | Combien d'arrêts jusqu'à ...? |
| | kom·byun da·ray zhews·ka ... |
| **Can you tell me when we get to ...?** | Pouvez-vous me dire quand nous arrivons à ...? |
| | poo·vay·voo mer deer kon noo za·ree·von a ... |
| **I want to get off at ...** | Je veux descendre à ... |
| | zher ver day·son·drer a ... |
| **I want to get off here.** | Je veux descendre ici. |
| | zher ver day·son·drer ee·see |

## Taxi

| | |
|---|---|
| **Where's the taxi stand?** | Où est la station de taxis? |
| | oo ay la sta·syon der tak·see |
| **I'd like a taxi at (nine o'clock).** | Je voudrais un taxi à (neuf heures). |
| | zher voo·dray un tak·see a (ner ver) |
| **Is your taxi free?** | Vous êtes libre? |
| | voo·zet lee·brer |
| **How much is it to ...?** | C'est combien pour aller à ...? |
| | say kom·byun poor a·lay a ... |
| **Please put the meter on.** | Mettez le compteur, s'il vous plaît. |
| | me·tay ler kon·ter seel voo play |

| | | |
|---|---|---|
| **Please take me to (this address).** | | Conduisez-moi à (cette adresse), s'il vous plaît. kon·dwee·zay mwa a (set a·dres) seel voo play |
| ✂ | **To ...** | À ... a ... |
| **Please slow down.** | | Roulez plus lentement, s'il vous plaît. roo·lay plew lont·mon seel voo play |
| **Please wait here.** | | Attendez ici, s'il vous plaît. a·ton·day ee·see seel voo play |
| **Stop at the corner.** | | Arrêtez-vous au coin de la rue. a·ray·tay voo o kwun der la rew |
| **Stop here.** | | Arrêtez-vous ici. a·ray·tay voo ee·see |

## Car & Motorbike

| | |
|---|---|
| **I'd like to hire a car.** | Je voudrais louer une voiture. zher voo·dray loo·way ewn vwa·tewr |
| **I'd like to hire a motorbike.** | Je voudrais louer une moto. zher voo·dray loo·way ewn mo·to |
| **How much for daily hire?** | Quel est le tarif par jour? kel ay ler ta·reef par zhoor |
| **How much for weekly hire?** | Quel est le tarif par semaine? kel ay ler ta·reef par ser·men |
| **Is this the road to ...?** | C'est la route pour ...? say la root poor ... |

## Fast Talk    Asking Questions

The easiest way to ask a 'yes/no' question in French is to make a statement with a rise in intonation. Alternatively, you can use *est-ce que* es·ker (lit: is-it that) in front of a statement.

The question words for more specific questions go at the start of the sentence: *comment* ko·mon (how), *qu'est-ce que* kes·ker (what), *quand* kon (when), *où* oo (where), *qui* kee (who) or *pourquoi* poor·kwa (why).

| | |
|---|---|
| **(How long) Can I park here?** | (Combien de temps) Est-ce que je peux stationner ici? (kom·byun der tom) es·ker zher per sta·syo·nay ee·see |
| **Where's a petrol station?** | Où est-ce qu'il y a une station-service? oo es·keel ya ewn sta·syon·ser·vees |

## Cycling

| | |
|---|---|
| **Where can I hire a bicycle?** | Où est-ce que je peux louer un vélo? oo es·ker zher per loo·way un vay·lo |
| **Are there cycling paths?** | Est-ce qu'il y a des pistes cyclables? es·keel ya day peest see·kla·bler |
| **Is there bicycle parking?** | Y a-t-il une zone de stationnement pour bicyclettes? ya·teel ewn zon der sta·syon·mon poor bee·see·klet |

AIRPORT & TRANSPORT

31

# Accommodation

## ⇒ Fast Phrases

| | |
|---|---|
| **I have a reservation.** | J'ai une réservation.<br>zhay ewn ray·zair·va·syon |
| **When/Where is breakfast served?** | Quand/Où le petit déjeuner est-il servi?<br>kon/oo ler per·tee day·zher·nay ay·teel sair·vee |
| **What time is checkout?** | Quand faut-il régler?<br>kon fo·teel ray·glay |

## Finding Accommodation

**PHRASE BUILDER**

| | | |
|---|---|---|
| **Where's a ...?** | Où est-ce qu'on peut trouver ...? | oo es·kon per troo·vay ... |
| bed and breakfast | une pension | ewn pon·syon |
| camping ground | un terrain de camping | un tay·run der kom·peeng |
| guesthouse | une pension | ewn pon·see·on |
| hotel | un hôtel | un o·tel |
| youth hostel | une auberge de jeunesse | ewn o·bairzh der zher·nes |

## Booking & Checking In

| | |
|---|---|
| **I have a reservation.** | J'ai une réservation.<br>zhay ewn ray·zair·va·syon |
| **Do you have a single room?** | Avez-vous une chambre à un lit?<br>a·vay·voo ewn shom·brer a un lee |
| **Do you have a double room?** | Avez-vous une chambre avec un grand lit?<br>a·vay·voo ewn shom·brer a·vek ung gron lee |
| **Do you have a twin room?** | Avez-vous une chambre avec des lits jumeaux?<br>a·vay·voo ewn shom·brer a·vek day lee zhew·mo |
| ✂ **Are there rooms?** | Y a-t-il des chambres?<br>ya·teel day shom·brer |
| **How much is it per night?** | Quel est le prix par nuit?<br>kel ay ler pree par nwee |
| **How much is it per person?** | Quel est le prix par personne?<br>kel ay ler pree par per·son |
| **How much is it per week?** | Quel est le prix par semaine?<br>kel ay ler pree par ser·men |
| **For (two) nights.** | Pour (deux) nuits.<br>poor (der) nwee |
| **From (July 2) to (July 6).** | Du (deux juillet) au (six juillet).<br>dew (der zhwee·yay) o (see zhwee·yay) |
| **Can I see it?** | Est-ce que je peux la voir?<br>es·ker zher per la vwar |
| **Is breakfast included?** | Le petit déjeuner est-il inclus?<br>ler per·tee day·zher·nay ay·teel un·klew |

> **Fast Talk**  **Using Patterns**
> Look out for patterns of words or phrases
> that stay the same, even when the situation changes,
> eg 'Do you have ...?' or 'I'd like to ...' (see p8). If you can
> recognise these patterns, you're already halfway to creating
> a full phrase. The dictionary will help you put other words
> together with these patterns to convey your meaning –
> even if it's not completely grammatically correct in all
> contexts, the dictionary form will always be understood.

| It's fine, I'll take it. | C'est bien, je la prends.<br>say byun zher la pron |
| Do I need to pay upfront? | Est-ce qu'il faut payer par avance?<br>es·keel fo pay·yay par a·vons |

## Requests & Questions

| When/Where is breakfast served? | Quand/Où le petit déjeuner est-il servi?<br>kon/oo ler per·tee day·zher·nay ay·teel sair·vee |
| Please wake me at (seven). | Réveillez-moi à (sept) heures, s'il vous plaît.<br>ray·vay·yay·mwa a (set) er seel voo play |
| Can I have my key, please? | Puis-je avoir ma clé, s'il vous plait?<br>pweezh av·war ma klay seel voo play |
| Can I use the kitchen? | Est-ce que je peux utiliser la cuisine?<br>es·ker zher per ew·tee·lee·zay la kwee·zeen |

| Can I use the telephone? | Est-ce que je peux utiliser le téléphone?<br>es·ker zher per ew·tee·lee·zay ler tay·lay·fon |
|---|---|
| Can I use the internet? | Est-ce que je peux utiliser l'Internet?<br>es·ker zher per ew·tee·lee·zay lun·tair·net |
| Do you have an elevator? | Avez-vous un ascenseur?<br>a·vay·voo un a·son·ser |
| Do you have a laundry service? | Avez-vous un service de blanchisserie?<br>a·vay·voo un sair·vees der blon·shees·ree |

### Local Knowledge — Hotels

| Can you recommend somewhere cheap? | Est-ce que vous pouvez recommander un logement pas cher?<br>es·ker voo poo·vay rer·ko·mon·day un lozh·mon pa shair |
|---|---|
| Can you recommend somewhere nearby? | Est-ce que vous pouvez recommander un logement près d'ici?<br>es·ker voo poo·vay rer·ko·mon·day un lozh·mon pray dee·see |
| Can you recommend somewhere romantic? | Est-ce que vous pouvez recommander un logement romantique?<br>es·ker voo poo·vay rer·ko·mon·day un lozh·mon ro·mon·teek |

| Do you have a safe? | Avez-vous un coffre-fort?<br>a·vay·voo ung ko·frer·for |
| **Do you change money here?** | Echangez-vous l'argent ici?<br>ay·shon·zhay·voo lar·zhon ee·see |
| **Do you arrange tours here?** | Organisez-vous des excursions ici?<br>or·ga·nee·zay·voo day zeks·kewr·syon ee·see |

## Complaints

| There's no hot water. | Il n'y a pas d'eau chaude.<br>eel nya pa do showd |

**PHRASE BUILDER**

| The ... doesn't work. | ... ne fonctionne pas. | ... ner fong·syon pa |
|---|---|---|
| air-conditioning | La climatisation | la klee·ma·tee·za·syon |
| heater | L'appareil de chauffage | la·pa·ray der sho·fazh |
| toilet | Les toilettes | lay twa·let |
| window | La fenêtre | la fer·ne·trer |

| It's too dark. | C'est trop sombre.<br>say tro som·brer |
| It's too noisy. | C'est trop bruyant.<br>say tro brew·yon |
| It's too small. | C'est trop petit.<br>say tro per·tee |

## PHRASE BUILDER

| Can I get another ...? | Est-ce que je peux avoir un/une autre ...? m/f | es·ker zher per a·vwar un/ewn o·trer ... |
|---|---|---|
| blanket | couverture f | koo·vair·tewr |
| pillow | oreiller m | o·ray·yay |
| sheet | drap m | drap |
| towel | serviette f | sair·vee·et |

## Checking Out

| What time is checkout? | Quand faut-il régler? kon fo·teel ray·glay |
|---|---|
| Can I leave my luggage here until (tonight)? | Puis-je laisser mes bagages jusqu'à (ce soir)? pweezh lay·say may ba·gazh zhews·ka (ser swar) |
| Can I have my deposit, please? | Est-ce que je pourrais avoir ma caution, s'il vous plaît? es·ker zher poo·ray a·vwar ma ko·syon seel voo play |
| Can I have my valuables, please? | Est-ce que je pourrais avoir mes biens précieux, s'il vous plaît? es·ker zher poo·ray a·vwar may byun pray·syer seel voo play |
| I had a great stay, thank you. | J'ai fait un séjour magnifique, merci. zhay fay un say·zhoor ma·nyee·feek mair·see |

# Eating & Drinking

## ⇒ Fast Phrases

| | |
|---|---|
| **Can I see the menu, please?** | Est-ce que je peux voir la carte, s'il vous plaît? es·ker zher per vwar la kart seel voo play |
| **I'd like a (beer), please.** | Je voudrais une (bière), s'il vous plaît. zher voo·dray ewn (byair) seel voo play |
| **Please bring the bill.** | Apportez-moi l'addition, s'il vous plaît. a·por·tay·mwa la·dee·syon seel voo play |

## Meals

| | |
|---|---|
| **breakfast** | petit déjeuner m per·tee day·zher·nay |
| **lunch** | déjeuner m day·zher·nay |
| **dinner** | dîner m dee·nay |
| **eat/drink** | manger/boire mon·zhay/bwar |

## Finding a Place to Eat

| | |
|---|---|
| **Can you recommend a bar?** | Est-ce que vous pouvez me conseiller un bar? es·ker voo poo·vay mer kon·say·yay um bar |
| **Can you recommend a cafe?** | Est-ce que vous pouvez me conseiller un café? es·ker voo poo·vay mer kon·say·yay ung ka·fay |
| **Can you recommend a restaurant?** | Est-ce que vous pouvez me conseiller un restaurant? es·ker voo poo·vay mer kon·say·yay un res·to·ron |
| **I'd like to reserve a table for (eight) o'clock.** | Je voudrais réserver une table pour (vingt) heures. zher voo·dray ray·zair·vay ewn ta·bler poor (vungt) er |
| **I'd like to reserve a table for (two) people.** | Je voudrais réserver une table pour (deux) personnes. zher voo·dray ray·zair·vay ewn ta·bler poor (der) pair·son |
| ✂ **For two, please.** | Pour deux, s'il vous plaît. poor der seel voo play |
| **I'd like a table in the (non)smoking area, please.** | Je voudrais une table dans un endroit pour (non·)fumeurs, s'il vous plaît. zher voo·dray ewn ta·bler don zun on·drwa poor (non·)few·mer seel voo play |

**Restaurants**

| | |
|---|---|
| **Where would you go for a cheap meal?** | Où est-ce qu'on trouve les restaurants bon marché? |
| | oo es kon troov lay res·to·ron bom mar·shay |
| **Where would you go for local specialities?** | Où est-ce qu'on trouve les spécialités locales? |
| | oo es kon troov lay spay·sya·lee·tay lo·kal |
| **Where would you go for a celebration?** | On va où pour faire la fête? |
| | on va oo poor fair la fet |

| | |
|---|---|
| **Are you still serving food?** | On peut toujours passer des commandes? |
| | om per too·zhoor pa·say day ko·mond |
| **How long is the wait?** | Il faut attendre combien de temps? |
| | eel fo a·ton·drer kom·byun der tom |

## Ordering & Paying

| | |
|---|---|
| **Can I see the menu, please?** | Est-ce que je peux voir la carte, s'il vous plaît? |
| | es·ker zher per vwar la kart seel voo play |
|  **Menu, please.** | La carte, s'il vous plaît. |
| | la kart seel voo play |

| What do you recommend? | Qu'est-ce que vous conseillez? kes·ker voo kon·say·yay |
|---|---|
| What's the local speciality? | Quelle est la spécialité locale? kel ay la spay·sya·lee·tay lo·kal |
| I'd like that one, please. | Je voudrais ça, s'il vous plaît. zher voo·dray sa seel voo play |
| I'd like the wine list, please. | Je voudrais la carte des vins, s'il vous plaît. zher voo·dray la kart day vun seel voo play |
| We're just having drinks. | C'est juste pour des boissons. say zhewst poor day bwa·son |
| ✂ Just drinks. | Juste des boissons. zhewst day bwa·son |

PHRASE BUILDER

| I'd like it ... | J'aime ça ... | zhem sa ... |
|---|---|---|
| medium | à point | a pwun |
| rare | saignant | say·nyon |
| steamed | à la vapeur | a la va·per |
| well-done | bien cuit | byun kwee |
| with (the dressing on the side) | avec (la sauce à côté) | a·vek (la sos a ko·tay) |
| without ... | sans ... | son ... |

| | |
|---|---|
| **Please bring (a glass).** | Apportez-moi (un verre), s'il vous plaît.<br>a·por·tay·mwa (un vair)<br>seel voo play |
| **I didn't order this.** | Ce n'est pas ce que j'ai commandé.<br>ser nay pa ser ker zhay ko·mon·day |
| **This is (too) cold.** | C'est (trop) froid.<br>say (tro) frwa |
| **That was delicious!** | C'était délicieux!<br>say·tay day·lee·syer |
| **Please bring the bill.** | Apportez-moi l'addition, s'il vous plaît.<br>a·por·tay·mwa la·dee·syon seel voo play |
| ✀ **Bill, please.** | L'addition, s'il vous plaît.<br>la·dee·syon seel voo play |
| **There's a mistake in the bill.** | Il y a une erreur dans la note.<br>eel ya ewn ay·rer don la not |

## Special Diets & Allergies

| | |
|---|---|
| **Is there a vegetarian restaurant near here?** | Y a-t-il un restaurant végétarien par ici?<br>ya·teel un res·to·ron vay·zhay·ta·ryun par ee·see |
| **Do you have vegetarian food?** | Vous faites les repas végétariens?<br>voo fet lay rer·pa vay·zhay·ta·ryun |

| I'm a vegan. | Je suis végétalien(ne). m/f |
| | zher swee vay·zhay·ta·lyun/ |
| | vay·zhay·ta·lyen |
| I'm a vegetarian. | Je suis végétarien(ne). m/f |
| | zher swee vay·zhay·ta·ryun/ |
| | vay·zhay·ta·ryen |
| I don't eat (red meat). | Je ne mange pas |
| | (la viande rouge). |
| | zher ner monzh pa |
| | (la vyond roozh) |
| Could you prepare a meal without butter? | Pouvez-vous préparer un repas sans beurre? |
| | poo·vay·voo pray·pa·ray un |
| | rer·pa son ber |
| Could you prepare a meal without eggs? | Pouvez-vous préparer un repas sans œufs? |
| | poo·vay·voo pray·pa·ray un |
| | rer·pa son zer |
| Could you prepare a meal without meat stock? | Pouvez-vous préparer un repas sans bouillon gras? |
| | poo·vay·voo pray·pa·ray un |
| | rer·pa son boo·yon gra |

EATING & DRINKING

## Fast Talk  Practising French

If you want to practise your language skills, try the waiters at a restaurant. Find your feet with straight-forward phrases such as asking for a table and ordering a drink, then initiate a conversation by asking for menu recommendations or asking how a dish is cooked. And as you'll often know food terms even before you've 'officially' learnt a word of the language, you're already halfway to understanding the response.

## PHRASE BUILDER

| I'm allergic to ... | Je suis allergique ... | zher swee za·lair·zheek ... |
|---|---|---|
| dairy produce | aux produits laitiers | o pro·dwee lay·tyay |
| fish | au poisson | o pwa·son |
| gluten | au gluten | o glew·ten |
| MSG | au glutamate de sodium | o glew·ta·mat der so·dyom |
| pork | au porc | o por |
| poultry | à la volaille | a la vo·lai |
| seafood | aux fruits de mer | o frwee der mair |
| shellfish | aux crustacés | o krew·sta·say |

## Nonalcoholic Drinks

| | |
|---|---|
| coffee (without sugar) | café (sans sucre) ka·fay (son sew·krer) |
| orange juice | jus d'orange zhew do·ronzh |
| soft drink | boisson non-alcoolisée bwa·son non·al·ko·lee·zay |
| tea (with milk) | thé (au lait) tay (o lay) |
| (mineral) water | eau (minérale) o (mee·nay·ral) |

## Alcoholic Drinks

| | |
|---|---|
| a shot of (gin) | un petit verre de (gin) um per·tee vair der (zheen) |

| a bottle of beer | une bouteille de bière<br>ewn boo·tay der byair |
| --- | --- |
| a glass of beer | un verre de bière<br>un vair der byair |
| a pint of beer | un demi de bière<br>un der·mee der byair |
| a bottle of ... wine | une bouteille de vin ...<br>ewn boo·tay der vun ... |

**PHRASE BUILDER**

| a glass of ... wine | un verre de vin ... | un vair der vun ... |
| --- | --- | --- |
| dessert | de dessert | der day·sair |
| red | rouge | roozh |
| rose | rosé | ro·zay |
| sparkling | mousseux | moo·ser |
| white | blanc | blong |

## In the Bar

| I'll buy you a drink. | Je vous offre un verre.<br>zher voo zo·frer un vair |
| --- | --- |
| What would you like? | Qu'est-ce que vous voulez?<br>kes·ker voo voo·lay |
| I'll have ... | Je prends ...<br>zher pron ... |
| Same again, please. | La même chose, s'il vous plaît.<br>la mem shoz seel voo play |
| It's my round. | C'est ma tournée.<br>say ma toor·nay |
| Cheers! | Santé!<br>son·tay |

## Buying Food

| | |
|---|---|
| **How much is (a kilo of cheese)?** | C'est combien (le kilo de fromage)?<br>say kom·byun (ler kee·lo der fro·mazh) |
| **Do you have other kinds?** | Est-ce que vous avez autre chose? **pol**<br>es ker voo za·vay o·trer shoz |
| **What's that?** | Qu'est-ce que c'est, ça?<br>kes·ker say sa |
| **Can I taste it?** | Je peux goûter?<br>zher per goo·tay |

PHRASE BUILDER

| I'd like ... | Je voudrais ... | zher voo·dray ... |
|---|---|---|
| **(200) grams** | (deux cents) grammes | (der son) gram |
| **(two) kilos** | (deux) kilos | (der) kee·lo |
| **(three) pieces** | (trois) morceaux | (trwa) mor·so |
| **(six) slices** | (six) tranches | (sees) tronsh |
| **some of that/those** | de ça | der sa |

| | |
|---|---|
| **Less.** | Moins.<br>mwun |
| **Enough.** | Ça ira.<br>sa ee·ra |
| **A bit more.** | Encore un peu.<br>ong·kor un per |

EATING & DRINKING

# Menu Decoder

This miniguide to French cuisine is designed to help you navigate menus. French nouns, and adjectives affected by gender, have their gender indicated by ⓜ or ⓕ. If it's a plural noun, you'll also see pl.

## - a -

**à la vapeur** a la va·per steamed
**abricot** ⓜ ab·ree·ko apricot
**agneau** ⓜ a·nyo lamb
**agneau de lait** ⓜ a·nyo der lay baby lamb
**ail** ⓜ ai garlic
**aloyau** ⓜ a·lwa·yo sirloin
**amandes** ⓕ pl a·mond almonds
**amuse-gueule** ⓜ a·mewz·gerl appetizer
**ananas** ⓜ a·na·nas pineapple
**anchois** ⓜ on·shwa anchovies
**andouille** ⓕ on·doo·yer sausage made of intestines
**aneth** ⓜ a·net dill
**anguille** ⓕ ong·gee·yer eel
**apéritif** ⓜ a·pay·ree·teef aperitif
**artichaut** ⓜ ar·tee·sho artichoke
**asperges** ⓕ a·spairzh asparagus
**au poivre** o pwa·vrer with pepper sauce
**aubergine** ⓕ o·bair·zheen eggplant
**avec** a·vek with
**avocat** ⓜ a·vo·ka avocado

## - b -

**banane** ⓕ ba·nan banana
**bar** ⓜ bar bass

**beignet** ⓜ be·nyay fritter
**betterave** ⓕ be·trav beetroot
**bière** ⓕ byair beer
**bifteck** ⓜ beef·tek beefsteak
**bisque** ⓕ beesk shellfish soup
**bœuf** ⓜ berf beef
**bœuf bourguignon** ⓜ berf boor·geen·yon beef stew with onions & mushrooms in a burgundy sauce
**bouillabaisse** ⓕ bwee·ya·bes fish soup from Marseilles
**bouilli(e)** ⓜ/ⓕ boo·yee boiled
**bouillon** ⓜ boo·yon broth
**bourride** ⓕ boo·reed Provençal white fish soup
**braisé(e)** ⓜ/ⓕ bre·se braised
**brème** ⓕ brem bream
**brochet** ⓜ bro·shay pike

## - c -

**cacahuètes** ⓕ pl ka·ka·wet peanuts
**caille** ⓕ kay·yer quail
**calmar** ⓜ kal·mar squid
**canard** ⓜ ka·nar duck
**canard sauvage** ⓜ ka·nar so·vazh wild duck
**caneton** ⓜ kan·ton duckling
**carbonnade** ⓕ kar·bo·nad selection of chargrilled meats

47

**carottes** ① pl ka·rot carrots
**carrelet** ⓜ ka·re·lay plaice
**cassis** ⓜ ka·sees blackcurrant
**céleri** ① sayl·ree celery
**cerfeuil** ⓜ ser·fer·yee chervil
**cerises** ① pl ser·rees cherries
**cervelle** ① sair·vel brains
**champignons** ⓜ pl shom·pee·nyon mushrooms
**châtaignes** ① pl sha·tayn·yer chestnuts
**chevreuil** ⓜ sher·vrer·yer venison
**chou** ⓜ shoo cabbage
**chou-fleur** ⓜ shoo·fler cauliflower
**choucroute** ① shoo·kroot pickled cabbage • sauerkraut
**ciboulette** ① see·boo·let chives
**citron** ⓜ see·tron lemon
**citrouille** ① see·troo·yer pumpkin
**cochon de lait** ⓜ ko·shon der lay suckling pig
**concombre** ⓜ kong·kom·brer cucumber
**consommé** ⓜ kon·so·may clear soup
**contre-filet** ⓜ kon·trer·fee·lay beef sirloin (steak)
**coq au vin** ⓜ kok o vun chicken cooked with wine, onions & mushrooms
**coquilles Saint-Jacques** ① pl ko·kee·yer sun·zhak scallops
**cornichon** ⓜ kor·nee·shon gherkin
**côtelette** ① kot·let cutlet
**coulis** ⓜ koo·lee fruit or vegetable purée
**courgette** ① koor·zhet zucchini
**crevettes grises** ① pl krer·vet grees shrimps
**crevettes roses** ① pl krer·vet ros prawns
**cru(e)** ⓜ/① krew raw

**crudités** ⓜ pl krew·dee·tay raw vegetableswith dressings
**cuisses de grenouilles** ① pl kwees de grer·noo·yer frogs' legs
**cuit(e)** ⓜ/① kwee(t) cooked
**cuit(e) au four** ⓜ/① kwee(t) o foor baked

## - d -

**darne** ⓜ darn fish cutlet
**datte** ① dat date
**daurade** ① do·rad sea bream
**dessert** ⓜ day·sair dessert
**dinde/dindon** ⓜ/① dund/dun·don turkey
**dindonneau** ⓜ dun·do·no young turkey
**doux/douce** ⓜ/① doo(s) mild • sweet
**du jour** dew zhoor of the day

## - e -

**écrevisses** ① pl ay·krer·vees crayfish
**émincé(e)** ⓜ/① ay·mun·say thinly sliced
**entré** ① on·tray entree
**entrecôte** ① on·trer·kot ribsteak
**épaule** ① ay·pol shoulder
**épinards** ⓜ pl ay·pee·nar spinach
**escargots** ⓜ pl es·kar·go snails
**estouffade** ① es·too·fad stew
**estragon** ⓜ es·tra·gon tarragon

## - f -

**faisan** ⓜ fer·zon pheasant
**fait(e) à la maison** ⓜ/① fe(t) a la may·zon homemade
**farci(e)** ⓜ/① far·see stuffed
**fenouil** ⓜ fer·noo·yer fennel
**figue** ① feeg fig

**filet** ⓜ fee·lay fillet
**flamiche** ⓕ fla·meesh leek quiche
**foie** ⓜ fwa liver
**fraises** ⓕ pl frez strawberries
**framboises** ⓕ pl from·bwaz raspberries
**fromage** ⓜ fro·mazh cheese
**fricassée** ⓕ free·ka·say stewed meat & vegetables in creamy sauce
**fumé(e)** ⓜ/ⓕ few·may smoked

## - g -

**gambas** ⓕ pl gom·bas king prawns
**garniture** ⓕ gar·nee·tewr garnish
**gelée** ⓕ zher·lay jelly
**gibier** ⓜ zheeb·yay game
**gigot** ⓜ zhee·go leg
**grillade** ⓕ gree·yad mixed grill
**grillé(e)** ⓜ/ⓕ gree·yay grilled
**groseilles** ⓕ pl gro·zay·yer gooseberries

## - h -

**hachis** ⓜ a·shee hash (chopped mince meat or vegetables)
**haricots verts** ⓜ pl a·ree·ko vair French or string beans
**homard** ⓜ o·mar Atlantic lobster
**huîtres** ⓜ pl wee·trer oysters

## - j -

**jambon** ⓜ zhom·bon ham

## - l -

**laitance** ⓕ lay·tons roe
**laitue** ⓕ lay·tew lettuce
**langoustines** ⓕ pl long·goo·steen scampi or Dublin Bay prawns
**langue** ⓕ long tongue

**lapin** ⓜ la·pun rabbit
**lard** ⓜ lar bacon
**laurier** ⓜ lo·ryay bay leaf
**légumes** ⓜ pl lay·gewm vegetables
**lentilles** ⓕ pl lon·tee·yer lentils
**lièvre** ⓜ lye·vrer hare
**longe** ⓕ lonzh loin
**lotte** ⓕ lot monkfish
**loup de mer** ⓜ loo de mer bass

## - m -

**maison** ⓕ may·zon of the house
**mange-tout** ⓜ monzh·too sugar peas • snowpeas
**maquereau** ⓜ ma·kro mackerel
**mariné(e)** ⓜ/ⓕ ma·ree·nay marinated
**marjolaine** ⓕ mar·zho·len marjoram
**marrons** ⓜ pl ma·ron chestnuts
**menthe** ⓕ mont mint
**menu dégustation** ⓜ mer·new day·gew·sta·syon tasting menu
**merguez** ⓕ mair·gez spicy red sausage
**merlan** ⓜ mer·lon whiting
**mirabelle** ⓕ mee·ra·bel plum
**moelle** ⓕ mwal bone marrow
**moules** ⓕ pl mool mussels
**moules marinières** ⓕ pl mool ma·ree·nyair mussels with shallots in white-wine sauce
**moutarde** ⓕ moo·tard mustard
**mûres** ⓕ pl mewr blackberries

## - n -

**noisettes** ⓕ pl nwa·zet hazelnuts
**noix** ⓕ nwa nuts • walnuts
**noix de coco** ⓕ nwa der ko·ko coconut

## - o -

**oie** ① wa goose
**oignon** ⓜ on·yon onion
**olives** ① pl o·leev olives
**orange** ① o·ronzh orange

## - p -

**palourdes** ① pl pa·loord clams
**pamplemousse** ⓜ pom·pler·moos grapefruit
**pané(e)** ⓜ/① pa·nay crumbed
**pastèque** ① pas·tek watermelon
**patate douce** ① pa·tat doos sweet potato
**pâté** ⓜ pa·tay paté • pie
**pâtes** ① pl pat pasta
**pêche** ① pesh peach
**persil** ⓜ pair·seel parsley
**petits pois** ⓜ pl per·tee pwa peas
**piquant** ⓜ pee·kon spicy hot
**pistou** ⓜ pee·stoo pesto
**plat** ⓜ **principal** pla prun·see·pal main course
**poché(e)** ⓜ/① po·shay poached
**poêlé(e)** ⓜ/① pwa·lay pan-fried
**poire** ① pwar pear
**poireau** ⓜ pwa·ro leek
**pois chiches** ⓜ pl pwa sheesh chickpeas
**poisson** ⓜ pwa·son fish
**poitrine de porc** ① pwa·treen de por pork belly
**poitrine de veau** ① pwa·treen de vo breast of veal
**poivre** ① pwa·vrer pepper
**poivron** ⓜ pwa·vron capsicum • pepper
**pomme** ① pom apple
**pomme de terre** ① pom der tair potato
**porc** ⓜ por pork
**potage** ⓜ po·tazh thick soup, usually vegetable

**potiron** ⓜ po·tee·ron pumpkin
**poularde** ① poo·lard fattened chicken
**poulet** ⓜ poo·lay chicken
**poulpe** ① poolp octopus
**prune** ① prewn plum
**pruneau** ⓜ prew·no prune

## - q -

**queue de bœuf** ① ker de berf oxtail

## - r -

**radis** ⓜ ra·dee radish
**ragoût** ⓜ ra·goo stew of meat or poultry & vegetables
**raifort** ⓜ ray·for horseradish
**raisins** ⓜ pl ray·zun grapes
**ratatouille** ① ra·ta·too·yer zucchini, eggplant, tomato & garlic dish
**rillettes** ① pl ree·yet potted meat (pork or goose)
**riz** ⓜ ree rice
**rognons** ⓜ pl ron·yon kidneys
**romarin** ⓜ ro·ma·run rosemary
**rôti(e)** ⓜ/① ro·tee roast

## - s -

**saint-pierre** ⓜ sun·pyair John Dory (fish)
**salade** ① sa·lad salad
**sanglier** ⓜ song·glee·yay wild boar
**sardines** ① pl sar·deen sardines
**sauge** ① sozh sage
**saumon** ⓜ so·mon salmon
**séché(e)** ⓜ/① say·shay dried
**sel** ⓜ sel salt
**selle** ① sel saddle (of meat)
**soupe** ① soop soup
**spiritueux** ⓜ pl spee·ree·twer spirits

**steak frites** ⓜ stek freet steak with chips
**steak tartare** ⓜ stek tar·tar raw minced beef, raw onion & egg yolk

## - t -

**thon** ⓜ ton tuna
**thym** ⓜ tun thyme
**topinambours** ⓜ pl to·pee·nom·boor Jerusalem artichokes
**tournedos** ⓜ toor·ner·do thick slices of fillet
**tourte** ⓕ toort pie
**tranché(e)** ⓜ/ⓕ tron·shay sliced
**tripes** ⓕ pl treep tripe

**truffes** ⓕ pl trewf truffles
**truite** ⓕ trweet trout

## - v -

**veau** ⓜ vo veal
**venaison** ⓕ ver·nay·zon venison
**vinaigre** ⓜ vee·nay·grer vinegar
**viande** ⓕ vyond meat
**vin blanc** ⓜ vum blong white wine
**vin de dessert** ⓜ vun der day·sair dessert wine
**vin mousseux** ⓜ vum moo·ser sparkling wine
**vin rouge** ⓜ vun roozh red wine
**volaille** ⓕ vo·lai poultry

# Sightseeing

## ⇒ Fast Phrases

| | |
|---|---|
| **When's the museum open?** | Le musée ouvre à quelle heure? ler mew·zay oo·vrer a kel er |
| **When's the next tour?** | C'est quand la prochaine excursion? say kon la pro·shen eks·kewr·syon |
| **Can I take photographs?** | Je peux prendre des photos? zher per pron·drer day fo·to |

## Planning

| | |
|---|---|
| **Do you have information on local sights?** | Avez-vous des renseignements sur les sites locaux à visiter? a·vay·voo day ron·sen·yer·mon sewr lay seet lo·ko a vee·zee·tay |
| **I have (one day).** | J'ai (un jour). zhay (un zhoor) |

| I'd like to see ... | J'aimerais voir ...<br>zhem·ray vwar ... |
|---|---|
| I'd like to hire a local guide. | Je voudrais faire appel aux services d'un guide.<br>zher voo·dray fair a·pel o sair·vees dung geed |
|  Are there guides? | Y a-t-il des guides?<br>ya·teel day geed |

## Questions

| What's that? | Qu'est-ce que c'est?<br>kes·ker say |
|---|---|
| How old is it? | Ça date de quand?<br>sa dat der kon |
| Who made it? | Qui l'a fait?<br>kee la fay |
| Can I take photographs? | Je peux prendre des photos?<br>zher per pron·drer day fo·to |
| Could you take a photo of me? | Pouvez-vous me prendre en photo?<br>poo·vay·voo mer pron·drer un fo·to |

PHRASE BUILDER

| I'd like a/an ... | Je voudrais ... | zher voo·dray ... |
|---|---|---|
| audio set | un écouteur | un ay·koo·ter |
| catalogue | un catalogue | ung ka·ta·log |
| guidebook (in English) | un guide (en anglais) | ung geed (on ong·lay) |
| local map | une carte de la région | ewn kart der la ray·zhyon |

## Getting In

| | |
|---|---|
| **What time does it open?** | Quelle est l'heure d'ouverture?<br>kel ay ler doo·vair·tewr |
| **What time does it close?** | Quelle est l'heure de fermeture?<br>kel ay ler der fer·mer·tewr |
| **What's the admission charge?** | Quel est le prix d'admission?<br>kel ay ler pree dad·mee·syon |

---

**PHRASE BUILDER**

| **Is there a discount for ...?** | Il y a une réduction pour les ...? | eel ya ewn ray·dewk·syon poor lay ... |
|---|---|---|
| **children** | enfants | zon·fon |
| **families** | familles | fa·mee·yer |
| **groups** | groupes | groop |
| **older people** | seniors | say·nyor |
| **students** | étudiants | zay·tew·dyon |

---

## Galleries & Museums

| | |
|---|---|
| **When's the gallery open?** | La galerie ouvre à quelle heure?<br>la gal·ree oo·vrer a kel er |
| **When's the museum open?** | Le musée ouvre à quelle heure?<br>ler mew·zay oo·vrer a kel er |
| **What's in the collection?** | Qu'est-ce qu'il y a dans la collection?<br>kes·keel·ya don la ko·lek·syon |
| **It's a/an ... exhibition.** | C'est une exposition ...<br>set ewn ek·spo·zee·syon ... |

**Fast Talk** **Forming Sentences**

You don't need to memorise complete sentences; instead, simply use key words to get your meaning across. For example, you might know that *quand* kon means 'when' in French. So if you've arranged a tour but don't know what time, just ask *Excursion quand?* eks·kewr·syon kon. Don't worry that you're not getting the whole sentence right – people will understand if you stick to the key words.

| I like the works of ... | J'aime l'œuvre de ... |
|---|---|
|  | zhem ler·vrer der ... |

### PHRASE BUILDER

| ... art | l'art ... | lar ... |
|---|---|---|
| contemporary | contemporain | kon·tom·po·run |
| impressionist | impressionniste | um·pray·syo·neest |
| modernist | moderniste | mo·dair·neest |
| Renaissance | de la Renaissance | der la rer·nay·sons |

## Tours

| When's the next tour? | C'est quand la prochaine excursion? |
|---|---|
|  | say kon la pro·shen eks·kewr·syon |
| Is food included? | Est-ce que la nourriture est incluse? |
|  | es·ker la noo·ree·tewr ay tung·klewz |

## Local Knowledge — Tours

| | |
|---|---|
| **Can you recommend a tour?** | Pouvez-vous me recommander une excursion?<br>poo·vay·voo mer rer·ko·mon·day ewn eks·kewr·syon |
| **Can you recommend a boat trip?** | Pouvez-vous me recommander une excursion en bateau?<br>poo·vay·voo mer rer·ko·mon·day ewn eks·kewr·syon om ba·to |
| **Can you recommend a day trip?** | Pouvez-vous me recommander une excursion d'une journée?<br>poo·vay·voo mer rer·ko·mon·day ewn eks·kewr·syon dewn zhoor·nay |

| | |
|---|---|
| **Is transport included?** | Est-ce que le transport est inclus?<br>es·ker ler trons·por ay tung·klew |
| **Do I need to take ...?** | Dois-je prendre ...?<br>dwa·zher pron·drer ... |
| **How long is the tour?** | L'excursion dure combien de temps?<br>leks·kewr·syon dewr kom·byun der tom |
| **What time should we be back?** | On doit rentrer pour quelle heure?<br>on dwa ron·tray poor kel er |
| **I've lost my group.** | J'ai perdu mon groupe.<br>zhay pair·dew mon groop |

# Shopping

## ⇒ Fast Phrases

| | |
|---|---|
| **Can I look at it?** | Est-ce que je peux le voir?<br>es·ker zher per ler vwar |
| **How much is it?** | C'est combien?<br>say kom·byun |
| **That's too expensive.** | C'est trop cher.<br>say tro shair |

## Looking For ...

| | |
|---|---|
| **Where's (a market)?** | Où est-ce qu'il y a (un marché)?<br>oo es·keel ya (un mar·shay) |
| **Where can I buy (locally produced goods)?** | Où puis-je acheter (des marchandises produits localement)?<br>oo pweezh ash·tay (day mar·shon·deez pro·dwee lo·kal·mon) |

## In the Shop

| | |
|---|---|
| **I'd like to buy ...** | Je voudrais acheter ...<br>zher voo·dray ash·tay ... |

57

## Shops

| | |
|---|---|
| **Where would you go for bargains?** | Où est-ce qu'on va pour des marchandises bon marché?<br>oo es·kon va poor day mar·shon·deez bom mar·shay |
| **Where would you go for souvenirs?** | Où est-ce qu'on va pour des souvenirs locales?<br>oo es·kon va poor day soov·neer lo·kal |

| | |
|---|---|
| **I'm just looking.** | Je regarde.<br>zher rer·gard |
| **Can I look at it?** | Est-ce que je peux le voir?<br>es·ker zher per ler vwar |
| **What is this made from?** | C'est fabriqué avec quoi?<br>say fa·bree·kay a·vek kwa |
| **Do you have any others?** | Vous en avez d'autres?<br>voo zon a·vay do·trer |
| **Does it have a guarantee?** | Est-ce qu'il y a une garantie?<br>es keel ya ewn ga·ron·tee |
| **It's faulty.** | C'est défectueux.<br>say day·fek·twer |
| **It's broken.** | C'est cassé.<br>say ka·say |
| **Can I have it wrapped?** | Pouvez-vous l'envelopper?<br>poo·vay·voo lon·vlo·pay |
| **Can I have it sent overseas?** | Pouvez-vous me l'envoyer à l'étranger?<br>poo·vay·voo mer lon·vwa·yay a lay·tron·zhay |

| Can I have a bag, please? | Puis-je avoir un sac, s'il vous plaît? pweezh a·vwar un sak seel voo play |
|---|---|
| I'd like my money back, please. | Je voudrais un remboursement, s'il vous plaît. zher voo·dray un rom·boors·mon seel voo play |
| I'd like to return this, please. | Je voudrais rapporter ceci, s'il vous plaît. zher voo·dray ra·por·tay ser·see seel voo play |

## Paying & Bargaining

| How much is it? | C'est combien? say kom·byun |
|---|---|
| ✂ How much? | Combien? kom·byun |
| It's (12) euros. | C'est (douze) euros. say (dooz) er·ro |
| Can you write down the price? | Pouvez-vous écrire le prix? poo·vay·voo ay·kreer ler pree |
| Can you lower the price? | Vous pouvez baisser le prix? voo poo·vay bay·say ler pree |
| That's too expensive. | C'est trop cher. say tro shair |
| Do you have something cheaper? | Avez-vous quelque chose de moins cher? a·vay·voo kel·ker shoz der mwun shair |
| I'll give you ... | Je vous donnerai ... zher voo don·ray ... |

## Fast Talk  False Friends

Some French words look like English words but have a different meaning altogether! For example, *car* kar is 'coach/bus' (not 'car', which is *voiture* vwa·tewr); *menu* me·new is 'set menu' (not 'menu', which is *carte* kart); *information* un·for·ma·syon is 'news' (not 'information', which is *renseignement* ron·sen·yer·mon); and *librairie* lee·bray·ree is 'bookshop' (not 'library', which is *bibliothèque* bee·blee·o·tek).

| | |
|---|---|
| Do you accept credit cards? | Est-ce que je peux payer avec une carte de crédit? es·ker zher per pay·yay a·vek ewn kart der kray·dee |
| I'd like my change, please. | Je voudrais ma monnaie, s'il vous plaît. zher voo·dray ma mo·nay seel voo play |
| Can I have a receipt, please? | Puis-je avoir un reçu, s'il vous plaît? pweezh a·vwar un rer·sew seel voo play |
| ✂ Receipt, please. | Un reçu, s'il vous plaît. un rer·sew seel voo play |

## Clothes & Shoes

| | |
|---|---|
| I'm looking for shoes. | Je cherche des chaussures. zher shairsh day sho·sewr |
| I'm looking for underwear. | Je cherche des sous-vêtements. zher shairsh day soo·vet·mon |

60

| My size is (medium). | Je fais du (moyen). |
| | zher fay dew (mwa·yen) |
| **Can I try it on?** | Puis-je l'essayer? |
| | pwee·zher lay·say·yay |
| **It doesn't fit.** | Ce n'est pas la bonne taille. |
| | ser nay pa la bon tai |
| **It's too big.** | C'est trop grand. |
| | say tro gron |
| **It's too small.** | C'est trop petit. |
| | say tro per·tee |

## Books & Reading

| **Is there an English-language bookshop?** | Y a-t-il une librairie de langue anglaise? |
| | ya·teel ewn lee·brair·ee der long ong·glayz |
| **Is there an English-language section?** | Y a-t-il un rayon anglais? |
| | ya·teel un ray·yon ong·glay |
| **Can you recommend a book for me?** | Pouvez-vous me conseiller un roman? |
| | poo·vay·voo mer kon·say·yay un ro·mon |
| **I'm looking for something by ...** | Je cherche quelque chose de ... |
| | zher shairsh kel·ker shoz der ... |
| **I'd like a dictionary.** | Je voudrais un dictionnaire. |
| | zher voo·dray un deek·syo·nair |
| **I'd like a newspaper (in English).** | Je voudrais un journal (en anglais). |
| | zher voo·dray un zhoor·nal (on ong·glay) |

**Fast Talk** **Money Slang**

You may hear these slang terms for 'money', so be prepared to recognise them: *blé* blay, *flouze* flooz, *pèze* pez or *pognon* po·nyon.

## Music & DVDs

| I'd like a CD/DVD. | Je voudrais un CD/DVD. zher voo·dray un say·day/ day·vay·day |
|---|---|
| I'd like some headphones. | Je voudrais un casque. zher voo·dray ung kask |
| What's his/her best recording? | Quel est son meilleur enregistrement? kel ay som may·yer on·rer·zhees·trer·mon |
| Can I listen to it here? | Je peux l'écouter ici? zher per lay·koo·tay ee·see |
| What region is this DVD for? | Pour quelle région ce DVD est-il codé? poor kel ray·zhyon ser day·vay·day ay·teel ko·day |

# Entertainment

## ≡ Fast Phrases

| | |
|---|---|
| **What's on tonight?** | Qu'est-ce qu'on joue ce soir?<br>kes·kon zhoo ser swar |
| **Where are the clubs?** | Où sont les clubs?<br>oo son lay klerb |
| **When will we meet?** | On se retrouve à quelle heure?<br>on ser rer·troov a kel er |
| **Where will we meet?** | On se retrouve où?<br>on ser rer·troov oo |

## Going Out

| | |
|---|---|
| **What's there to do in the evenings?** | Qu'est-ce qu'on peut faire le soir?<br>kes·kon per fair ler swar |
| **What's on today?** | Qu'est-ce qu'on joue aujourd'hui?<br>kes·kon zhoo o·zhoor·dwee |
| **What's on tonight?** | Qu'est-ce qu'on joue ce soir?<br>kes·kon zhoo ser swar |
|  **What's on?** | Qu'est-ce qu'on joue?<br>kes·kon zhoo |

**Fast Talk** **Conversation Dos & Don'ts**

Sport and culture are safe areas of conversation and food is a sure way to get a French person speaking, but money talk (prices, income etc) is best avoided.

| | | |
|---|---|---|
| **What's on this weekend?** | Qu'est-ce qu'on joue ce week-end? | kes·kon zhoo ser wee·kend |
| **Is there a local entertainment guide?** | Y a-t-il un programme des spectacles? | ya·teel un pro·gram day spek·ta·kler |
| **Is there a local gay guide?** | Y a-t-il un guide des endroits gais? | ya·teel un geed day zon·drwa gay |

PHRASE BUILDER

| **I'd like to go to a/the ...** | Je voudrais aller ... | zher voo·dray a·lay ... |
|---|---|---|
| ballet | au ballet | o ba·lay |
| bar | au bar | o bar |
| cafe | au café | o ka·fay |
| cinema | au cinéma | o see·nay·ma |
| concert | à un concert | a ung kon·sair |
| nightclub | en boîte | on bwat |
| opera | à l'opéra | a lo·pay·ra |
| pub | au pub | o perb |
| restaurant | au restaurant | o res·to·ron |
| theatre | au théâtre | o tay·a·trer |

## Local Knowledge   Clubs

| | |
|---|---|
| **Can you recommend clubs?** | Pouvez-vous me recommander des clubs?<br>poo·vay·voo mer<br>rer·ko·mon·day day klerb |
| **Can you recommend gay venues?** | Pouvez-vous me recommander des boîtes gaies?<br>poo·vay·voo mer<br>rer·ko·mon·day day bwat gay |
| **Can you recommend pubs?** | Pouvez-vous me recommander des pubs?<br>poo·vay·voo mer<br>rer·ko·mon·day day perb |

## Meeting Up

| | |
|---|---|
| **When shall we meet?** | On se retrouve à quelle heure?<br>on ser rer·troov a kel er |
| **Let's meet at (eight o'clock).** | On peut se retrouver à (huit heures).<br>on per ser rer·troo·vay a (wee ter) |
| **Where will we meet?** | On se retrouve où?<br>on ser rer·troov oo |
| **Let's meet at (the entrance).** | On peut se retrouver devant (l'entrée).<br>on per ser rer·troo·vay der·von (lon·tray) |
| **I'll pick you up.** | Je viendrai te chercher.<br>zher vyun·dray ter shair·shay |
| **Sorry I'm late.** | Désolé d'être en retard.<br>day·zo·lay de·trer on rer·tar |

# Practicalities

## ≡ Fast Phrases

| | |
|---|---|
| **Where's the nearest ATM?** | Où est le guichet automatique le plus proche? oo ay ler gee·shay o·to·ma·teek ler plew prosh |
| **Is there wireless internet access here?** | Avez-vous le wifi ici? a·vay·voo ler wee·fee ee·see |
| **Where are the toilets?** | Où sont les toilettes? oo son lay twa·let |

## Banking

| | |
|---|---|
| **Where's a bank?** | Où est-ce qu'il y a une banque? oo es·keel ya ewn bongk |
| **What time does the bank open?** | À quelle heure ouvre la banque? a kel er oo·vrer la bongk |
| **Where's the nearest ATM?** | Où est le guichet automatique le plus proche? oo ay ler gee·shay o·to·ma·teek ler plew prosh |
| **Where's the nearest foreign exchange office?** | Où est le bureau de change le plus proche? oo ay ler bew·ro der shonzh ler plew prosh |

| Where can I (change money)? | Où est-ce que je peux (changer de l'argent)?<br>oo es·ker zher per (shon·zhay der lar·zhon) |
|---|---|
| I'd like to (withdraw money). | Je voudrais (retirer de l'argent).<br>zher voo·dray (rer·tee·ray der lar·zhon) |
| What's the exchange rate? | Quel est le taux de change?<br>kel ay ler to der shonzh |
| What's the charge for that? | Quel est le tarif pour cela?<br>kel ay ler ta·reef poor ser·la |

## Phone/Mobile Phone

| Where's the nearest public phone? | Où est le téléphone public le plus proche?<br>oo ay ler tay·lay·fon pewb·leek ler plew prosh |
|---|---|
| I'd like to buy a phonecard. | Je voudrais acheter une carte téléphonique.<br>zher voo·dray ash·tay ewn kart tay·lay·fo·neek |
| I want to make a call to (Singapore). | Je veux téléphoner à (Singapour).<br>zher ver tay·lay·fo·nay a (sung·ga·poor) |
| I want to make a reverse-charge/collect call. | Je veux téléphoner en PCV.<br>zher ver tay·lay·fo·nay om pay·say·vay |

| | |
|---|---|
| **How much is a (three)-minute call?** | Quel est le prix d'une communication de (trois) minutes?<br>kel ay ler pree dewn ko·mew·nee·ka·syon der (trwa) mee·newt |
| **The number is ...** | Le numéro est ...<br>ler new·may·ro ay ... |
| **I've been cut off.** | J'ai été coupé(e). m/f<br>zhay ay·tay koo·pay |
| **It's busy.** | La ligne est occupée.<br>la lee·nyer ay to·kew·pay |
| **I'd like a charger for my phone.** | Je voudrais un chargeur pour mon portable.<br>zher voo·dray un shar·zher poor mom por·ta·bler |
| **I'd like a SIM card for the network.** | Je voudrais une carte SIM pour le réseau.<br>zher voo·dray ewn kart seem poor ler ray·zo |

## Internet

| | |
|---|---|
| **Where's the local internet cafe?** | Où est le cybercafé du coin?<br>oo ay ler see·bair·ka·fay dew kwun |
| **Is there wireless internet access here?** | Avez-vous le wifi ici?<br>a·vay·voo ler wee·fee ee·see |
| **Can I connect my laptop here?** | Est-ce que je peux utiliser mon ordinateur portable ici?<br>es·ker zher per ew·tee·lee·zay mong or·dee·na·ter por·ta·bler ee·see |

| **Do you have headphones (with a microphone)?** | Avez-vous un casque (avec un micro)? a·vay·voo ung kask (a·vek ung mee·kro) |
|---|---|

| I'd like to ... | Je voudrais ... | zher voo·dray ... |
|---|---|---|
| burn a CD | brûler un CD | brew·lay un se·de |
| check my email | consulter mon courrier | kon·sewl·tay mong koo·ryay |
| download my photos | télécharger mes photos | tay·lay·shar·zhay may fo·to |
| use a printer | utiliser une imprimante | ew·tee·lee·zay ewn um·pree·mont |
| use a scanner | utiliser un scanner | ew·tee·lee·zay un ska·nair |
| use Skype | utiliser Skype | ew·tee·lee·zay skaip |

| **How much per hour?** | C'est combien l'heure? say kom·byun ler |
|---|---|
| **How much per page?** | C'est combien la page? say kom·byun la pazh |
| **How do I log on?** | Comment faire pour me connecter? ko·mon fair poor mer ko·nek·tay |
| **It's crashed.** | C'est tombé en panne. say tom·bay om pan |
| **I've finished.** | J'ai terminé. zhay tair·mee·nay |

| Can I connect (my camera) to this computer? | Est-ce que je peux brancher (mon appareil photo) sur cet ordinateur? |
| | es·ker zher per bron·shay (mong na·pa·ray fo·to) sewr set or·dee·na·ter |

## Emergencies

| Help! | Au secours! |
| | o skoor |
| Stop! | Arrêtez! |
| | a·ray·tay |
| Go away! | Allez-vous-en! |
| | a·lay·voo·zon |
| Leave me alone! | Laissez-moi tranquille! |
| | lay·say·mwa trong·keel |
| Thief! | Au voleur! |
| | o vo·ler |

PRACTICALITIES

### Fast Talk — Understanding French

Most sentences are composed of several words (or parts of words) serving various grammatical functions, as well as those that carry meaning (primarily nouns and verbs). If you're finding it hard to understand what someone is saying to you, listen out for the nouns and verbs to work out the context – this shouldn't be hard as they are usually more emphasised in speech. If you're still having trouble, a useful phrase to know is *Pourriez-vous parler plus lentement, s'il vous plaît?* poo·ree·yay voo par·lay plew lon·ter·mon seel voo play (Could you please speak more slowly?).

| | | |
|---|---|---|
| **Fire!** | Au feu! | o fer |
| **Watch out!** | Faites attention! | fet a·ton·syon |
| **It's an emergency!** | C'est urgent! | say tewr·zhon |
| **There's been an accident.** | Il y a eu un accident. | eel ya ew un ak·see·don |
| **Call the police!** | Appelez la police! | a·play la po·lees |
| **Call a doctor!** | Appelez un médecin! | a·play un mayd·sun |
| **Do you have a first-aid kit?** | Avez-vous une trousse de première urgence? | a·vay·voo ewn troos der prer·myair ewr·zhons |
| **Can you help me, please?** | Est-ce que vous pourriez m'aider, s'il vous plaît? | es·ker voo poo·ryay may·day seel voo play |
| **Please help me!** | Aidez-moi, s'il vous plaît! | ay·day·mwa seel voo play |
| **Can I use the telephone?** | Est-ce que je pourrais utiliser le téléphone? | es·ker zher poo·ray ew·tee·lee·zay ler tay·lay·fon |
| **Where are the toilets?** | Où sont les toilettes? | oo son lay twa·let |
| **I'm lost.** | Je suis perdu(e). m/f | zher swee pair·dew |

## Police

| Where's the police station? | Où est le commissariat de police? |
| | oo ay ler ko·mee·sar·ya der po·lees |
| I've been raped. | J'ai été violé(e). m/f |
| | zhay ay·tay vyo·lay |
| I've been robbed. | On m'a volé. |
| | on ma vo·lay |
| I've lost (my bags). | J'ai perdu (mes valises). |
| | zhay pair·dew (may va·leez) |
| I've lost (my passport). | J'ai perdu (mon passeport). |
| | zhay pair·dew (mom pas·por) |
| (My money) was stolen. | On m'a volé (mon argent). |
| | on ma vo·lay (mon ar·zhon) |
| I want to contact my embassy. | Je veux contacter mon ambassade. |
| | zher ver kon·tak·tay mon om·ba·sad |
| I want to contact my consulate. | Je veux contacter mon consulat. |
| | zher ver kon·tak·tay mon kon·sew·la |
| I have insurance. | J'ai une assurance. |
| | zhay ewn a·sew·rons |

## Health

| Where's a nearby chemist? | Où y a-t-il une pharmacie par ici? |
| | oo ya·teel ewn far·ma·see par ee·see |

72

| | | |
|---|---|---|
| **Where's a nearby dentist?** | Où y a-t-il un dentiste par ici? | oo ya·teel un don·teest par ee·see |
| **Where's a nearby hospital?** | Où y a-t-il un hôpital par ici? | oo ya·teel un o·pee·tal par ee·see |
| **I need a doctor (who speaks English).** | J'ai besoin d'un médecin (qui parle anglais). | zhay ber·zwun dun mayd·sun (kee parl ong·glay) |
| **Could I see a female doctor?** | Est-ce que je peux voir une femme médecin? | es·ker zher per vwar ewn fam mayd·sun |
| **I'm sick.** | Je suis malade. | zher swee ma·lad |
| **It hurts here.** | J'ai une douleur ici. | zhay ewn doo·ler ee·see |
| **I've been vomiting.** | J'ai vomi. | zhay vo·mee |
| **I feel nauseous.** | J'ai des nausées. | zhay day no·zay |
| **I feel dizzy.** | J'ai des frissons. | zhay day free·son |

### PHRASE BUILDER

| **I have (a/an) ...** | J'ai ... | zhay ... |
|---|---|---|
| cold | un rhume | un rewm |
| diarrhoea | la diarrhée | la dya·ray |
| fever | de la fièvre | der la fyay·vrer |
| headache | mal à la tête | mal a la tet |
| infection | une infection | ewn un·fek·syon |
| toothache | mal aux dents | mal o don |

**Fast Talk**  **Addressing People**

The French can seem very formal about addressing people they don't know. They use *Monsieur* mer·syer (Mr), *Madame* ma·dam (Ms/Mrs) or *Mademoiselle* mad·mwa·zel (Miss) where English speakers would use no term of address at all.

| | |
|---|---|
| **I'm on medication for ...** | Je prends des médicaments pour ... zher pron day may·dee·ka·mon poor ... |
| **I need something for ...** | J'ai besoin d'un médicament pour ... zhay ber·zwun dun may·dee·ka·mom poor ... |
| **My prescription is ...** | Mon ordonnance indique ... mon or·do·nons on·deek ... |
| **I'm allergic (to antibiotics).** | Je suis allergique (aux antibiotiques). zher swee za·lair·zheek (o zon·tee·byo·teek) |
| **I have a skin allergy.** | J'ai une allergie de peau. zhay ewn a·lair·zhee der po |

# *Dictionary*

## ENGLISH *to* FRENCH

*anglais – français*

Nouns in this dictionary have their gender indicated by ⓜ or ⓕ.
If it's a plural noun, you'll also see pl. Where a word that could be
either a noun or a verb has no gender indicated, it's a verb.

## ~ *a* ~

**accommodation** logement ⓜ
lozh·mon
**account** compte ⓜ kont
**afternoon** après-midi ⓜ
a·pray·mee·dee
**air-conditioned** climatisé
kee·ma·tee·zay
**airplane** avion ⓜ a·vyon
**airport** aéroport ⓜ a·ay·ro·por
**alarm clock** réveil ⓜ ray·vay
**alcohol** alcool ⓜ al·kol
**appointment** rendez-vous ⓜ
ron·day·voo
**arrivals** arrivées ⓕ a·ree·vay
**art gallery** galerie ⓕ gal·ree
**ashtray** cendrier ⓜ son·dree·yay

**at** à a
**ATM** guichet ⓜ automatique de
banque (GAB) gee·shay o·to·ma·teek
der bonk
**autumn** automne ⓜ o·ton

## ~ *b* ~

**B&W (film)** noir et blanc nwar ay
blong
**baby** bébé ⓜ bay·bay
**back (body)** dos ⓜ do
**backpack** sac ⓜ à dos sak a do
**bad** mauvais(e) ⓜ/ⓕ mo·vay(z)
**bag** sac ⓜ sak
**baggage** bagages ⓜ ba·gazh
**baggage allowance** franchise ⓕ
fron·sheez

75

**baggage claim** retrait ⓜ des bagages rer·tray day ba·gazh

**bakery** boulangerie ⓕ boo·lon·zhree

**Band-Aid** sparadrap ⓜ spa·ra·dra

**bank** banque ⓕ bongk

**bank account** compte ⓜ bancaire kont bong·kair

**bath** baignoire ⓕ be·nywar

**bathroom** salle ⓕ de bain sal der bun

**battery** pile ⓕ peel

**beach** plage ⓕ plazh

**beautiful** beau/belle ⓜ/ⓕ bo/bel

**beauty salon** salon ⓜ de beauté sa·lon der bo·tay

**bed** lit ⓜ lee

**bed linen** draps ⓜ dra

**bedroom** chambre ⓕ à coucher shom·brer a koo·shay

**beer** bière ⓕ byair

**bicycle** vélo ⓜ vay·lo

**big** grand(e) ⓜ/ⓕ gron(d)

**bill (restaurant)** addition ⓕ a·dee·syon

**birthday** anniversaire ⓜ a·nee·vair·sair

**blanket** couverture ⓕ koo·vair·tewr

**blood group** groupe ⓜ sanguin groop song·gun

**boarding house** pension ⓕ pon·syon

**boarding pass** carte ⓕ d'embarquement kart dom·bar·ker·mon

**boat** bateau ⓜ ba·to

**book** livre ⓜ leev·rer

**book (make a booking)** réserver ray·zair·vay

**booked up** complet/complète ⓜ/ⓕ kom·play/kom·plet

**bookshop** librairie ⓕ lee·bray·ree

**border** frontière ⓕ fron·tyair

**bottle** bouteille ⓕ boo·tay

**box** boîte ⓕ bwat

**boy** garçon ⓜ gar·son

**boyfriend** petit ami ⓜ per·tee ta·mee

**bra** soutien-gorge ⓜ soo·tyung·gorzh

**brakes** freins ⓜ frun

**bread** pain ⓜ pun

**briefcase** serviette ⓕ sair·vyet

**broken** cassé(e) ⓜ/ⓕ ka·say

**brother** frère ⓜ frair

**brown** brun/brune ⓜ/ⓕ brun/brewn

**building** bâtiment ⓜ ba·tee·mon

**bus (city)** (auto)bus ⓜ (o·to·)bews

**bus (intercity)** (auto)car ⓜ (o·to·)kar

**bus station** gare ⓕ routière gar roo·tyair

**bus stop** arrêt ⓜ d'autobus a·ray do·to·bews

**business** affaires ⓕ a·fair

**business class** classe ⓕ affaires klas a·fair

**busy** occupé(e) ⓜ/ⓕ o·kew·pay

**butcher's shop** boucherie ⓕ boosh·ree

## ~ C ~

**cafe** café ⓜ ka·fay

**call** appeler a·play

**camera** appareil ⓜ photo a·pa·ray fo·to

**can (tin)** boîte ⓕ bwat

**cancel** annuler a·new·lay

**car** voiture ⓕ vwa·tewr

**car hire** location ⓕ de voitures lo·ka·syon der vwa·tewr

**car owner's title** carte grise ⓕ kart greez

**car registration** immatriculation ee·ma·tree·kew·la·syon

**cash** argent ⓜ ar·zhon

**cashier** caissier/caissière ⓜ/ⓕ kay·syay/kay·syair

**chairlift (skiing)** télésiège ⓜ tay·lay·syezh

**change** changer shon·zhay

**change (coins)** monnaie ⓕ mo·nay

**change (money)** échanger
ay·shon·zhay

**check (banking)** chèque ⓜ shek

**check (bill)** addition ⓕ a·dee·syon

**check-in (desk)** enregistrement
on·rer·zhee·strer·mon

**cheque (banking)** chèque ⓜ shek

**child** enfant ⓜ&ⓕ on·fon

**church** église ⓕ ay·gleez

**cigarette lighter** briquet ⓜ bree·kay

**city** ville ⓕ veel

**city centre** centre-ville ⓜ son·trer·veel

**clean** propre pro·prer

**cleaning** nettoyage ⓜ net·wa·yazh

**cloakroom** vestiaire ⓜ vays·tyair

**closed** fermé(e) ⓜ/ⓕ fair·may

**clothing** vêtements ⓜ vet·mon

**coat** manteau ⓜ mon·to

**coffee** café ⓜ ka·fay

**coins** pièces ⓕ pyes

**cold** froid(e) ⓜ/ⓕ frwa(d)

**comfortable** confortable
kon·for·ta·bler

**company** entreprise ⓕ on·trer·preez

**computer** ordinateur ⓜ or·dee·na·ter

**condom** préservatif ⓜ
pray·zair·va·teef

**confirm (a booking)** confirmer
kon·feer·may

**connection** rapport ⓜ ra·por

**convenience store** supérette ⓕ de
quartier sew·pay·ret der kar·tyay

**cook** cuire kweer

**cool** frais/fraîche ⓜ/ⓕ fray/fresh

**cough** toux ⓕ too

**countryside** campagne ⓕ
kom·pa·nyer

**cover charge** couvert ⓜ koo·vair

**crafts** artisanat ⓜ ar·tee·za·na

**credit card** carte ⓕ de crédit kart der
kray·dee

**currency exchange** taux ⓜ de
change to der shonzh

**customs** douane ⓕ dwan

## -d-

**daily** quotidien(ne) ⓜ/ⓕ
ko·tee·dyun/ko·tee·dyen

**date (day)** date ⓕ dat

**date of birth** date ⓕ de naissance
dat der nay·sons

**daughter** fille ⓕ fee·yer

**day** jour ⓜ zhoor

**day after tomorrow** après-demain
a·pray·der·mun

**day before yesterday** avant-hier
a·von·tyair

**delay** retard ⓜ rer·tar

**delicatessen** charcuterie ⓕ
shar·kew·tree

**depart (leave)** partir par·teer

**department store** grand magasin ⓜ
gron ma·ga·zun

**departure** départ ⓜ day·par

**deposit** dépôt ⓜ day·po

**diaper** couche ⓕ koosh

**dictionary** dictionnaire ⓜ
deek·syo·nair

**dinner** dîner ⓜ dee·nay

**direct** direct(e) ⓜ/ⓕ dee·rekt

**dirty** sale sal

**discount** remise ⓕ rer·meez

**dish** plat ⓜ pla

**doctor** médecin ⓜ mayd·sun

**dog** ⓜ chien shyun

**double bed** grand lit ⓜ gron lee

**double room** chambre ⓕ pour
deux personnes shom·brer poor der
pair·son

**dress** robe ⓕ rob

**drink** boire bwar

**drink (alcoholic)** verre ⓜ vair

**drink (beverage)** boisson ⓕ bwa·son

**drivers licence** permis ⓜ de conduire
pair·mee der kon·dweer

**drunk** ivre ee·vrer

**dry** sec/sèche ⓜ/ⓕ sek/sesh

77

## -e-

**each** chaque shak
**early** tôt to
**east** est ⓜ est
**eat** manger mon·zhay
**economy class** classe ⓕ touriste klas too·reest
**elevator** ascenseur ⓜ a·son·ser
**embassy** ambassade ⓕ om·ba·sad
**English** anglais(e) ⓜ/ⓕ ong·glay(z)
**enough** assez a·say
**entry** entrée ⓕ on·tray
**envelope** enveloppe ⓕ on·vlop
**evening** soir ⓜ swar
**every** chaque shak
**everything** tout too
**excess (baggage)** excédent ek·say·don
**exchange** échanger ay·shon·zhay
**exhibition** exposition ⓕ ek·spo·zee·syon
**exit** sortie ⓕ sor·tee
**expensive** cher/chère ⓜ/ⓕ shair
**express (mail)** exprès eks·pres

## -f-

**fall (autumn)** automne ⓜ o·ton
**family** famille ⓕ fa·mee·yer
**fare** tarif ⓜ ta·reef
**fashion** mode ⓕ mod
**fast** rapide ra·peed
**father** père ⓜ pair
**ferry** bac ⓜ bak
**fever** fièvre ⓕ fyev·rer
**film (for camera)** pellicule ⓕ pay·lee·kewl
**fine (penalty)** amende ⓕ a·mond
**finger** doigt ⓜ dwa
**first class** première classe ⓕ prer·myair klas
**fish shop** poissonnerie ⓕ pwa·son·ree

**fleamarket** marché ⓜ aux puces mar·shay o pews
**flight** vol ⓜ vol
**floor (storey)** étage ⓜ ay·tazh
**flu** grippe ⓕ greep
**footpath** sentier ⓜ son·tyay
**foreign** étranger/étrangère ⓜ/ⓕ ay·tron·zhay/ay·tron·zhair
**forest** forêt ⓕ fo·ray
**free (available)** disponible dees·po·nee·bler
**free (gratis)** gratuit(e) ⓜ/ⓕ gra·twee(t)
**fresh** frais/fraîche ⓜ/ⓕ fray/fresh
**friend** ami/amie ⓜ/ⓕ a·mee

## -g-

**garden** jardin ⓜ zhar·dun
**gas (for cooking)** gaz ⓜ gaz
**gas (petrol)** essence ⓕ e·sons
**gift** cadeau ⓜ ka·do
**girl** fille ⓕ fee·yer
**girlfriend** petite amie ⓕ per·teet a·mee
**glasses (spectacles)** lunettes ⓕ pl lew·net
**gloves** gants ⓜ pl gon
**go** aller a·lay
**go out** sortir sor·teer
**gold** or ⓜ or
**grateful** reconnaissant(e) ⓜ/ⓕ rer·ko·nay·son(t)
**grocery** épicerie ⓕ ay·pee·sree
**guesthouse** pension ⓕ (de famille) pon·syon (der fa·mee·yer)
**guided tour** visite ⓕ guidée vee·zeet gee·day

## -h-

**half** moitié ⓕ mwa·tyay
**handsome** beau/belle ⓜ/ⓕ bo/bel

**heated** chauffé(e) ⓜ/ⓕ sho·fay
**help** aider ay·day
**here** ici ee·see
**highway** autoroute ⓕ o·to·root
**hire** louer loo·ay
**holidays** vacances ⓕ pl va·kons
**honeymoon** lune ⓕ de miel lewn
der myel
**hospital** hôpital ⓜ o·pee·tal
**hot** chaud(e) ⓜ/ⓕ show(d)
**hotel** hôtel ⓜ o·tel
**hour** heure ⓕ er
**husband** mari ⓜ ma·ree

## ~ i ~

**identification card (ID)** carte ⓕ
d'identité kart dee·don·tee·tay
**ill** malade ma·lad
**included** compris(e) ⓜ/ⓕ kom·pree(z)
**information** renseignements ⓜ pl
ron·sen·yer·mon
**insurance** assurance ⓕ a·sew·rons
**intermission** entracte ⓜ on·trakt
**internet cafe** cybercafé ⓜ
see·bair·ka·fay
**interpreter** interprète ⓜ/ⓕ
un·tair·pret
**itinerary** itinéraire ⓜ ee·tee·nay·rair

## ~ j ~

**jacket** veste ⓕ yest
**jeans** jean ⓜ zheen
**jewellery** bijoux ⓜ pl bee·zhoo
**journey** voyage ⓜ vwa·yazh
**jumper (sweater)** pull ⓜ pewl

## ~ k ~

**key** clé ⓕ klay
**kind (nice)** gentil(le) ⓜ/ⓕ zhon·tee
**kitchen** cuisine ⓕ kwee·zeen

## ~ l ~

**last (previous)** dernier/dernière ⓜ/ⓕ
dair·nyay/dair·nyair
**late** en retard on rer·tar
**later** plus tard plew·tar
**launderette** laverie ⓕ lav·ree
**laundry (place)** blanchisserie ⓕ
blon·shees·ree
**laundry (clothes)** linge ⓜ lunzh
**leather** cuir ⓜ kweer
**left luggage (office)** consigne ⓕ
kon·see·nyer
**letter** lettre ⓕ lay·trer
**lift (elevator)** ascenseur ⓜ a·son·ser
**linen (material)** lin ⓜ lun
**linen (sheets etc)** linge ⓜ lunzh
**locked** fermé(e) à clé ⓜ/ⓕ fair·may
a klay
**lost** perdu(e) ⓜ/ⓕ pair·dew
**lost property office** bureau ⓜ des
objets trouvés bew·ro day zob·zhay
troo·vay
**luggage** bagages ⓜ pl ba·gazh
**luggage lockers** consigne ⓕ
automatique kon·see·nyer o·to·ma·teek
**lunch** déjeuner ⓜ day·zher·nay

## ~ m ~

**mail (postal system)** poste ⓕ post
**make-up** maquillage ⓜ ma·kee·yazh
**man** homme ⓜ om
**manager (restaurant, hotel)**
gérant(e) ⓜ/ⓕ zhay·ron(t)
**map (of country)** carte ⓕ kart
**map (of town)** plan ⓜ plon
**market** marché ⓜ mar·shay
**meal** repas ⓜ rer·pa
**meat** viande ⓕ vyond
**medicine (medication)** médicament
ⓜ may·dee·ka·mon
**metro station** station ⓕ de métro

sta·syon der may·tro
**midday** midi mee·dee
**midnight** minuit mee·nwee
**milk** lait ⓜ lay
**mineral water** eau ⓕ minérale o
mee·nay·ral
**mobile phone** téléphone ⓜ portable
tay·lay·fon por·ta·bler
**modem** modem ⓜ mo·dem
**money** argent ⓜ ar·zhon
**month** mois ⓜ mwa
**morning** matin ⓜ ma·tun
**mother** mère ⓕ mair
**motorcycle** moto ⓕ mo·to
**motorway (tollway)** autoroute ⓕ
o·to·root
**mountain** montagne ⓕ mon·ta·nyer
**museum** musée ⓜ mew·zay
**music shop** disquaire ⓜ dee·skair

## ~ n ~

**name** nom ⓜ nom
**napkin** serviette ⓕ sair·vyet
**nappy (diaper)** couche ⓕ koosh
**newsagent** marchand ⓜ de journaux
mar·shon der zhoor·no
**newspaper** journal ⓜ zhoor·nal
**next (month)** prochain(e) ⓜ/ⓕ
pro·shun/pro·shen
**night** nuit ⓕ nwee
**night out** soirée ⓕ swa·ray
**nightclub** boîte ⓕ bwat
**no vacancy** complet kom·play
**nonsmoking** non-fumeur non·few·mer
**noon** midi mee·dee
**north** nord ⓜ nor
**now** maintenant mun·ter·non
**number** numéro ⓜ new·may·ro

## ~ o ~

**oil** huile ⓕ weel

**oil (petrol)** pétrole ⓜ pay·trol
**one-way (ticket)** (billet) simple
(bee·yay) sum·pler
**open** ouvert(e) ⓜ/ⓕ oo·vair(t)
**opening hours** heures ⓕ pl
d'ouverture lay zer doo·vair·tewr
**orange (colour, fruit)** orange o·ronzh

## ~ p ~

**painter** peintre ⓜ pun·trer
**painting (a work)** tableau ⓜ ta·blo
**painting (the art)** peinture ⓕ
pun·tewr
**pants** pantalon ⓜ pon·ta·lon
**pantyhose** collant ⓜ ko·lon
**paper** papier ⓜ pa·pyay
**party (night out)** soirée ⓕ swa·ray
**passenger** voyageur/voyageuse ⓜ/ⓕ
vwa·ya·zher/vwa·ya·zherz
**passport** passeport ⓜ pas·por
**passport number** numéro ⓜ de
passeport new·may·ro der pas·por
**path** chemin ⓜ shmun
**penknife** canif ⓜ ka·neef
**pensioner** retraité(e) ⓜ/ⓕ
rer·tray·tay
**petrol** essence ⓕ e·sons
**petrol station** station-service ⓕ
sta·syon·sair·vees
**phone book** annuaire ⓜ an·wair
**phone box** cabine ⓕ téléphonique
ka·been tay·lay·fo·neek
**phone card** télécarte ⓕ tay·lay·kart
**phrasebook** recueil ⓜ d'expressions
rer·ker·yer dek·spray·syon
**picnic** pique-nique ⓜ peek·neek
**pillow** oreiller ⓜ o·ray·yay
**pillowcase** taie ⓕ d'oreiller tay
do·ray·yay
**platform** quai ⓜ kay
**play (theatre)** pièce ⓕ de théâtre
pyes der tay·a·trer
**police officer (in city)** policier ⓜ

po·lee·syay
**police officer (in country)**
gendarme ⓜ zhon·darm
**police station** commissariat ⓜ
ko·mee·sar·ya
**post code** code ⓜ postal kod pos·tal
**post office** bureau ⓜ de poste bew·ro
der post
**postcard** carte postale ⓕ kart
pos·tal
**pound (money, weight)** livre ⓕ
leev·rer
**prescription** ordonnance ⓕ
or·do·nons
**present (gift)** cadeau ⓜ ka·do
**price** prix ⓜ pree

## - q -

**quiet** tranquille trong·keel

## - r -

**receipt** reçu ⓜ rer·sew
**refund** remboursement ⓜ
rom·boor·ser·mon
**rent** louer loo·ay
**repair** réparer ray·pa·ray
**return** revenir rerv·neer
**return (ticket)** aller retour ⓜ a·lay
rer·toor
**road** route ⓕ root
**room** chambre ⓕ shom·brer
**room number** numéro ⓜ de chambre
new·may·ro der shom·brer

## - s -

**safe** coffre-fort ⓜ kof·rer·for
**sea** mer ⓕ mair
**season** saison ⓕ say·zon
**seat (place)** place ⓕ plas
**seatbelt** ceinture ⓕ de sécurité

sun·tewr der say·kew·ree·tay
**self service** libre-service ⓜ
lee·brer·sair·vees
**service** service ⓜ sair·vees
**service charge** service ⓜ sair·vees
**share (a dorm etc)** partager
par·ta·zhay
**share with** partager avec par·ta·zhay
a·vek
**shirt** chemise ⓕ sher·meez
**shoe** chaussure ⓕ sho·sewr
**shop** magasin ⓜ ma·ga·zun
**shopping centre** centre ⓜ
commercial son·trer ko·mair·syal
**short (height)** court(e) ⓜ/ⓕ koor(t)
**show** montrer mon·tray
**shower** douche ⓕ doosh
**sick** malade ma·lad
**silk** soie ⓕ swa
**silver** argent ⓜ ar·zhon
**single (person)** célibataire
say·lee·ba·tair
**single room** chambre ⓕ pour
une personne shom·brer poor ewn
pair·son
**sister** sœur ⓕ ser
**size (general)** taille ⓕ tai
**skirt** jupe ⓕ zhewp
**sleeping bag** sac ⓜ de couchage sak
der koo·shazh
**sleeping car** wagon-lit ⓜ va·gon·lee
**slide (film)** diapositive ⓕ
dya·po·zee·teev
**smoke** fumée ⓕ few·may
**snack** casse-croûte ⓜ kas·kroot
**snow** neige ⓕ nezh
**socks** chaussettes ⓕ sho·set
**son** fils ⓜ fees
**soon** bientôt byun·to
**south** sud ⓜ sewd
**spring (season)** printemps ⓜ
prun·tom
**square (town)** place ⓕ plas
**stairway** escalier ⓜ es·ka·lyay

**stamp** timbre ⓜ tum·brer
**stationer's (shop)** papeterie ⓕ
pa·pet·ree
**stolen** volé(e) ⓜ/ⓕ vo·lay
**street** rue ⓕ rew
**student** étudiant(e) ⓜ/ⓕ
ay·tew·dyon(t)
**subtitles** sous-titres ⓜ soo·tee·trer
**suitcase** valise ⓕ va·leez
**summer** été ⓜ ay·tay
**supermarket** supermarché ⓜ
sew·pair·mar·shay
**surface mail (land)** voie de terre
vwa der tair
**surface mail (sea)** voie maritime
vwa ma·ree·teem
**surname** nom ⓜ de famille nom der
fa·mee·yer
**sweater** pull ⓜ pewl
**swim** nager na·zhay
**swimming pool** piscine ⓕ pee·seen

## ~ t ~

**taxi stand** station ⓕ de taxi sta·syon
der tak·see
**ticket** billet ⓜ bee·yay
**ticket machine** distributeur ⓜ de
tickets dee·stree·bew·ter der tee·kay
**ticket office** guichet ⓜ gee·shay
**time** temps ⓜ tom
**timetable** horaire ⓜ o·rair
**tip (gratuity)** pourboire ⓜ
poor·bwar
**to** à a
**today** aujourd'hui o·zhoor·dwee
**together** ensemble on·som·bler
**tomorrow** demain der·mun
**tour** voyage ⓜ vwa·yazh
**tourist office** office de tourisme ⓜ
o·fees·der too·rees·mer
**towel** serviette ⓕ sair·vyet
**train station** gare ⓕ gar
**transit lounge** salle ⓕ de transit sal

der tron·zeet
**travel agency** agence ⓕ de voyage
a·zhons der vwa·yazh
**travellers cheque** chèque ⓜ de
voyage shek der vwa·yazh
**trousers** pantalon ⓜ pon·ta·lon
**twin beds** lits ⓜ pl jumeaux lee
zhew·mo

## ~ u ~

**underwear** sous-vêtements ⓜ
soo·vet·mon
**urgent** urgent(e) ⓜ/ⓕ ewr·zhon(t)

## ~ v ~

**vacancy** chambre ⓕ libre shom·brer
lee·brer
**vacant** libre lee·brer
**vacation** vacances ⓕ pl va·kons
**validate** valider va·lee·day
**vegetable** légume ⓜ lay·gewm
**view** vue ⓕ vew

## ~ w ~

**waiting room** salle ⓕ d'attente sal
da·tont
**walk** marcher mar·shay
**warm** chaud(e) ⓜ/ⓕ sho(d)
**wash (something)** laver la·vay
**washing machine** machine ⓕ à laver
ma·sheen a la·vay
**watch** montre ⓜ mon·trer
**water** eau ⓕ o
**week** semaine ⓕ ser·men
**west** ouest ⓜ west
**when** quand kon
**where** où oo
**which** quel(le) ⓜ/ⓕ kel
**which** qui kee
**white** blanc/blanche ⓜ/ⓕ blong/

blonsh

**who** qui kee
**why** pourquoi poor·kwa
**wife** femme ① fam
**window** fenêtre ① fer·nay·trer
**wine** vin ⓜ vun
**winter** hiver ⓜ ee·vair
**without** sans son
**woman** femme ① fam
**wool** laine ① len

## ~ y ~

**year** année ⓜ a·nay
**yes** oui wee
**yesterday** hier ee·yair
**you** sg inf tu tew
**you** sg pol & pl vous voo
**youth hostel** auberge ① de jeunesse
o·bairzh der zher·nes

# Dictionary

## FRENCH *to* ENGLISH

*français – anglais*

Nouns in this dictionary have their gender indicated by ⓜ or ⓕ. If it's a plural noun, you'll also see pl. Where a word that could be either a noun or a verb has no gender indicated, it's a verb.

## - a -

**à** a at • to

**addition** ⓕ a·dee·syon bill • check

**aéroport** ⓜ a·ay·ro·por airport

**affaires** ⓕ a·fair business

**agence** ⓕ **de voyage** a·zhons der vwa·yazh travel agency

**agence** ⓕ **immobilière** a·zhons ee·mo·bee·lyair estate agency

**aider** ay·day help

**alcool** ⓜ al·kol alcohol

**aller** a·lay go

**aller et retour** ⓜ a·lay ay rer·toor return (ticket)

**ambassade** ⓕ om·ba·sad embassy

**amende** ⓕ a·mond fine (penalty)

**ami(e)** ⓜ/ⓕ a·mee friend

**anglais(e)** ⓜ/ⓕ ong·glay(z) English

**année** ⓜ a·nay year

**anniversaire** ⓜ a·nee·vair·sair birthday

**annuaire** ⓜ an·wair phone book

**annuler** a·new·lay cancel

**antiquité** ⓕ on·tee·kee·tay antique

**appareil** ⓜ **photo** a·pa·ray fo·to camera

**appeler** a·play call

**après-demain** a·pray·der·mun day after tomorrow

**après-midi** ⓜ a·pray·mee·dee afternoon

**argent** ⓜ ar·zhon cash • money • silver

**arrêt** ⓜ **d'autobus** a·ray do·to·bews bus stop

**arrivées** ⓕ a·ree·vay arrivals

**artisanat** ⓜ ar·tee·za·na crafts

**ascenseur** ⓜ a·son·ser elevator • lift
**assez** a·say enough
**assurance** ⓕ a·sew·rons insurance
**Attention!** a·ton·syon Careful!
**auberge** ⓕ **de jeunesse** o·bairzh der zher·nes youth hostel
**aujourd'hui** o·zhoor·dwee today
**auto** ⓕ o·to car
**automne** ⓜ o·ton autumn • fall
**autoroute** ⓕ o·to·root highway • motorway
**avant-hier** a·von·tyair day before yesterday
**avion** ⓜ a·vyon aeroplane

## ~ b ~

**bac** ⓜ bak ferry
**bagages** ⓜ pl ba·gazh baggage • luggage
**baignoire** ⓕ be·nywar bath
**banque** ⓕ bongk bank
**bateau** ⓜ ba·to boat
**bâtiment** ⓜ ba·tee·mon building
**beau/belle** ⓜ/ⓕ bo/bel beautiful • handsome
**bébé** ⓜ bay·bay baby
**bientôt** byun·to soon
**bière** ⓕ byair beer
**bijoux** ⓜ pl bee·zhoo jewellery
**billet** ⓜ bee·yay ticket
**— simple** sum·pler one-way ticket
**blanc/blanche** ⓜ/ⓕ blong/blonsh white
**bleu(e)** ⓜ/ⓕ bler blue
**boire** bwar drink
**boisson** ⓕ bwa·son drink (beverage)
**boîte** ⓕ bwat box • can (tin) • carton (for ice cream) • nightclub
**boucherie** ⓕ boosh·ree butcher's shop
**boulangerie** ⓕ boo·lon·zhree bakery
**bouteille** ⓕ boo·tay bottle
**briquet** ⓜ bree·kay cigarette lighter
**brun/brune** ⓜ/ⓕ brun/brewn brown

**bureau** ⓜ bew·ro office
**— de poste** der post post office
**— des objets trouvés** day zob·zhay troo·vay lost property office
**bus** ⓜ bews bus (city)

## ~ c ~

**cabine** ⓕ **téléphonique** ka·been tay·lay·fo·neek phone box
**cadeau** ⓜ ka·do gift • present
**café** ⓜ ka·fay cafe • coffee
**caissier/caissière** ⓜ/ⓕ kay·syay/kay·syair cashier • teller
**campagne** ⓕ kom·pa·nyer countryside
**canif** ⓜ ka·neef penknife
**car** ⓜ kar bus (intercity)
**carte** ⓕ kart map (of country)
**— de crédit** kart der kray·dee credit card
**— d'embarquement** kart dom·bar·ker·mon boarding pass
**— d'identité** kart dee·don·tee·tay identification card (ID)
**— grise** kart greez car owner's title
**— postale** kart pos·tal postcard
**cassé(e)** ⓜ/ⓕ ka·say broken
**casse-croûte** ⓜ kas·kroot snack
**ceinture** ⓕ **de sécurité** sun·tewr der say·kew·ree·tay seatbelt
**célibataire** say·lee·ba·tair single (person)
**cendrier** ⓜ son·dree·yay ashtray
**centre** ⓜ **commercial** son·trer ko·mair·syal shopping centre
**centre-ville** ⓜ son·trer·veel city centre
**chambre** ⓕ shom·brer room
**— à coucher** a koo·shay bedroom
**— libre** lee·brer vacancy
**— pour deux personnes** poor der pair·son double room
**— pour une personne** poor ewn pair·son single room
**changer** shon·zhay change
**chaque** shak each • every

**chaud(e)** ⓜ/ⓕ show(d) hot • warm
**chauffé(e)** ⓜ/ⓕ sho·fay heated
**chaussettes** ⓕ sho·set socks
**chaussure** ⓕ sho·sewr shoe
**chemin** ⓜ shmun path • lane • way
**chemise** ⓕ sher·meez shirt
**chèque** ⓜ shek check (banking) • cheque
— **de voyage** der vwa·yazh travellers cheque
**cher/chère** ⓜ/ⓕ shair expensive • dear
**chercher** shair·shay look for
**chien** ⓜ shyun dog
**cimetière** ⓕ seem·tyair cemetery
**cirque** ⓜ seerk circus
**classe affaires** ⓕ klas a·fair business class
**classe touriste** ⓕ klas too·reest economy class
**clé** ⓕ klay key
**climatisé** kee·ma·tee·zay air-conditioned
**code** ⓜ **postal** kod pos·tal post code
**coffre-fort** ⓜ kof·rer·for safe
**collant** ⓜ ko·lon pantyhose
**commissariat** ⓜ ko·mee·sar·ya police station
**complet/complète** ⓜ/ⓕ kom·play/kom·plet booked up • no vacancy
**compris(e)** ⓜ/ⓕ kom·pree(z) included
**compte** ⓜ kont account
— **bancaire** bong·kair bank account
**confirmer** kon·feer·may confirm (a booking)
**confortable** kon·for·ta·bler comfortable
**consigne** ⓕ kon·see·nyer left luggage (office)
— **automatique** o·to·ma·teek luggage lockers
**couche** ⓕ koosh diaper • nappy
**court(e)** ⓜ/ⓕ koor(t) short (height)
**couvert** ⓜ koo·vair cover charge
**couverture** ⓕ koo·vair·tewr blanket
**cuir** ⓜ kweer leather

**cuisine** ⓕ kwee·zeen kitchen
**cuisinier/cuisinière** ⓜ/ⓕ kwee·zee·nyay/kwee·zee·nyair cook
**cybercafé** ⓜ see·bair·ka·fay internet cafe

## - d -

**date** ⓕ **de naissance** dat der nay·sons date of birth
**déjeuner** ⓜ day·zher·nay lunch
**demain** der·mun tomorrow
— **après-midi** a·pray·mee·dee tomorrow afternoon
— **matin** ma·tun tomorrow morning
— **soir** swar tomorrow evening
**départ** ⓜ day·par departure
**dépôt** ⓜ day·po deposit
**dernier/dernière** ⓜ/ⓕ dair·nyay/dair·nyair last (previous)
**diapositive** ⓕ dya·po·zee·teev slide (film)
**dictionnaire** ⓜ deek·syo·nair dictionary
**dîner** ⓜ dee·nay dinner
**direct(e)** ⓜ/ⓕ dee·rekt direct
**disquaire** ⓜ dee·skair music shop
**distributeur** ⓜ **de tickets** dee·stree·bew·ter der tee·kay ticket machine
**doigt** ⓜ dwa finger
**dos** ⓜ do back (body)
**douane** ⓕ dwan customs
**douche** ⓕ doosh shower
**draps** ⓜ dra bed linen

## - e -

**eau** ⓕ o water
— **minérale** mee·nay·ral mineral water
**échange** ⓜ ay·shonzh exchange
**échanger** ay·shon·zhay change (money) • exchange
**église** ⓕ ay·gleez church

**en retard** on rer·tar late
**enfant** ⓜ&ⓕ on·fon child
**enregistrement**
on·rer·zhee·strer·mon check-in (desk)
**ensemble** on·som·bler together
**entracte** ⓜ on·trakt intermission
**entrée** ⓕ on·tray entry
**entreprise** ⓕ on·trer·preez company
**enveloppe** ⓕ on·vlop envelope
**épicerie** ⓕ ay·pee·sree grocery
**escalier** ⓜ es·ka·lyay stairway
**essence** ⓕ ay·sons gas • petrol
**est** ⓜ est east
**étage** ⓜ ay·tazh floor (storey)
**été** ⓜ ay·tay summer
**étranger/étrangère** ⓜ/ⓕ
ay·tron·zhay/ay·tron·zhair foreign •
stranger
**étudiant(e)** ⓜ/ⓕ ay·tew·dyon(t)
student
**excédent** ek·say·don excess
(baggage)
**exposition** ⓕ ek·spo·zee·syon
exhibition
**exprès** eks·pres express (mail)

## - f -

**faire les courses** fair lay koors go
shopping
**famille** ⓕ fa·mee·yer family
**félicitations** fay·lee·see·ta·syon
congratulations
**femme** ⓕ fam wife • woman
**fenêtre** ⓕ fer·nay·trer window
**fermé(e)** ⓜ/ⓕ fair·may closed
**— à clé** a klay locked
**fièvre** ⓕ fyev·rer fever
**fille** ⓕ fee·yer daughter • girl
**fils** ⓜ fees son
**forêt** ⓕ fo·ray forest
**frais/fraîche** ⓜ/ⓕ fray/fresh cool •
fresh
**franchise** ⓕ fron·sheez baggage
allowance
**freins** ⓜ frun brakes

**frère** ⓜ frair brother
**froid(e)** ⓜ/ⓕ frwa(d) cold
**frontière** ⓕ fron·tyair border
**fumer** few·may smoke

## - g -

**gants** ⓜ pl gon gloves
**garçon** ⓜ gar·son boy
**gare** ⓕ gar train station
**— routière** roo·tyair bus station
**gaz** ⓜ gaz gas (for cooking)
**gendarme** ⓜ zhon·darm police
officer (in country)
**gentil(le)** ⓜ/ⓕ zhon·tee kind • nice
**gérant(e)** ⓜ/ⓕ zhay·ron(t) manager
(restaurant, hotel)
**grand(e)** ⓜ/ⓕ gron(d) big • large •
tall
**grand lit** ⓜ gron lee double bed
**grand magasin** ⓜ gron ma·ga·zun
department store
**gratuit(e)** ⓜ/ⓕ gra·twee(t) free
(gratis)
**grippe** ⓕ greep flu
**gris(e)** ⓜ/ⓕ gree(z) gray • grey
**groupe** ⓜ **sanguin** groop song·gun
blood group
**guichet** ⓜ gee·shay ticket office
**— automatique de banque (GAB)**
o·to·ma·teek der bonk ATM

## - h -

**heure** ⓕ er hour • time
**heures** ⓕ pl **d'ouverture** er
doo·vair·tewr opening hours
**hier** ee·yair yesterday
**hiver** ⓜ ee·vair winter
**homme** ⓜ om man
**hôpital** ⓜ o·pee·tal hospital
**horaire** ⓜ o·rair timetable
**hors service** or sair·vees out of order
**hôtel** ⓜ o·tel hotel
**huile** ⓕ weel oil

## -i-

**ici** ee·see here

**immatriculation** ee·ma·tree·kew·la·syon car registration

**interprète** m/f un·tair·pret interpreter

**itinéraire** m ee·tee·nay·rair itinerary • route

**ivre** ee·vrer drunk

## -j-

**jardin** m zhar·dun garden

**jean** m zheen jeans

**jour** m zhoor day

**journal** m zhoor·nal newspaper

**jupe** f zhewp skirt

## -l-

**laine** f len wool

**lait** m lay milk

**laver** la·vay wash (something)

**laverie** f lav·ree launderette

**légume** m lay·gewm vegetable

**lettre** f lay·trer letter

**librairie** f lee·bray·ree bookshop

**libre** lee·brer free (at liberty) • vacant

**libre-service** m lee·brer·sair·vees self service

**lin** m lun linen (material)

**linge** m lunzh laundry (clothes) • linen

**lit** m lee bed

**lits** m pl **jumeaux** lee zhew·mo twin beds

**livre** m leev·rer book

**livre** f leev·rer pound (money, weight)

**location** f **de voitures** lo·ka·syon der vwa·tewr car hire

**logement** m lozh·mon accommodation

**louer** loo·ay hire • rent

**lune** f **de miel** lewn der myel honeymoon

**lunettes** f pl lew·net glasses (spectacles)

## -m-

**machine** f **à laver** ma·sheen a la·vay washing machine

**magasin** m ma·ga·zun shop

**magnétoscope** m ma·nyay·to·skop video recorder

**maintenant** mun·ter·non now

**malade** ma·lad ill • sick

**manger** mon·zhay eat

**manteau** m mon·to coat

**maquillage** m ma·kee·yazh make-up

**marchand de journaux** m mar·shon der zhoor·no newsagent

**marché** m mar·shay market

**— aux puces** o pews fleamarket

**marcher** mar·shay walk

**mari** m ma·ree husband

**matin** m ma·tun morning

**mauvais(e)** m/f mo·vay(z) bad • off (meat) • wrong (direction)

**médecin** m mayd·sun doctor

**médicament** m may·dee·ka·mon medicine (medication)

**mer** f mair sea

**mère** f mair mother

**midi** mee·dee midday • noon

**minuit** mee·nwee midnight

**mode** f mod fashion

**mois** m mwa month

**moitié** f mwa·tyay half

**monnaie** f mo·nay change (coins)

**montagne** f mon·ta·nyer mountain

**montre** f mon·trer watch

**moto** f mo·to motorcycle

**musée** m mew·zay art gallery • museum

## - n -

**nager** na·zhay swim
**neige** ① nezh snow
**nettoyage** ⑩ net·wa·yazh cleaning
**nettoyer** net·wa·yay clean
**Noël** ⑩ no·el Christmas
**noir(e)** ⑩/① nwar black
**noir et blanc** nwar ay blong B&W (film)
**nom** ⑩ nom name
**— de famille** der fa·mee·yer surname
**non-fumeur** non·few·mer non-smoking
**nord** ⑩ nor north
**nuit** ① nwee night
**numéro** ⑩ new·may·ro number
**— de chambre** der shom·brer room number
**— de passeport** der pas·por passport number

## - o -

**occupé(e)** ⑩/① o·kew·pay busy
**office de tourisme** ⑩ o·fees·der too·rees·mer tourist office
**or** ⑩ or gold
**orange** o·ronzh orange (colour, fruit)
**ordinateur** ⑩ or·dee·na·ter computer
**— portable** por·ta·bler laptop
**ordonnance** ① or·do·nons prescription
**oreiller** ⑩ o·ray·yay pillow
**où** oo where
**ouest** ⑩ west west
**ouvert(e)** ⑩/① oo·vair(t) open

## - p -

**pain** ⑩ pun bread
**palais** ⑩ pa·lay palace
**pantalon** ⑩ pon·ta·lon pants • trousers

**papeterie** ① pa·pet·ree stationer's (shop)
**papier** ⑩ pa·pyay paper
**partager** par·ta·zhay share
**partir** par·teer depart • leave
**passeport** ⑩ pas·por passport
**peintre** ⑩ pun·trer painter
**peinture** ① pun·tewr painting (the art)
**pellicule** ① pay·lee·kewl film (for camera)
**pension** ⑩ pon·syon boarding house • bed & breakfast
**— de famille** der fa·mee·yer guesthouse
**perdu(e)** ⑩/① pair·dew lost
**père** ⑩ pair father
**permis de conduire** ⑩ pair·mee der kon·dweer drivers licence
**petit ami** ⑩ per·tee a·mee boyfriend
**petite ami** ① per·teet a·mee girlfriend
**pièce** ① **de théâtre** pyes der tay·a·trer play (theatre)
**pièce** ① **d'identité** pyes dee·don·tee·tay identification
**pièces** ① pyes coins
**pile** ① peel battery
**pique-nique** ⑩ peek·neek picnic
**piscine** ① pee·seen swimming pool
**place** ① plas seat (place) • square (town)
**plage** ① plazh beach
**plan** ⑩ plon map (of town)
**plat** ⑩ pla dish
**plus tard** plew·tar later
**poissonnerie** ① pwa·son·ree fish shop
**policier** ⑩ po·lee·syay police officer (in city)
**poste** ① post mail (postal system)
**pourboire** ⑩ poor·bwar tip (gratuity)
**pourquoi** poor·kwa why
**première classe** ① prer·myair klas first class

**prénom** ⓜ pray·non first name
**préservatif** ⓜ pray·zair·va·teef condom
**printemps** ⓜ prun·tom spring (season)
**prix** ⓜ pree price
**prochain(e)** ⓜ/ⓕ pro·shun/pro·shen next (month)
**pull** ⓜ pewl jumper • sweater

~ *q* ~

**quai** ⓜ kay platform
**quand** kon when
**quel/quelle** ⓜ/ⓕ kel what • which
**qui** kee which • who
**quotidien(ne)** ⓜ/ⓕ ko·tee·dyun/ ko·tee·dyen daily

~ *r* ~

**rapide** ra·peed fast • quick
**rapport** ⓜ ra·por connection
**reconnaissant(e)** ⓜ/ⓕ rer·ko·nay·son(t) grateful
**reçu** ⓜ rer·sew receipt
**recueil** ⓜ **d'expressions** rer·ker·yer dek·spray·syon phrasebook
**remboursement** ⓜ rom·boor·ser·mon refund
**remise** ⓕ rer·meez discount
**rendez-vous** ⓜ ron·day·voo appointment • date
**renseignements** ⓜ pl ron·sen·yer·mon information
**réparer** ray·pa·ray repair
**repas** ⓜ rer·pa meal
**réserver** ray·zair·vay book (make a booking)
**retard** ⓜ rer·tar delay
**retrait** ⓜ **des bagages** rer·tray day ba·gazh baggage claim
**retraité(e)** ⓜ/ⓕ rer·tray·tay pensioner • retired
**réveil** ⓜ ray·vay alarm clock

**revenir** rerv·neer return
**robe** ⓕ rob dress
**rose** roz pink
**rouge** roozh red
**route** ⓕ root road
**rue** ⓕ rew street

~ *s* ~

**sac** ⓜ sak bag
**— à dos** a do backpack
**— de couchage** der koo·shazh sleeping bag
**saison** ⓕ say·zon season
**sale** sal dirty
**salle** ⓕ sal room
**— d'attente** sal da·tont waiting room
**— de bain** sal der bun bathroom
**— de transit** sal der tron·zeet transit lounge
**salon** ⓜ **de beauté** sa·lon der bo·tay beauty salon
**sans** son without
**sec/sèche** ⓜ/ⓕ sek/sesh dry
**semaine** ⓕ ser·men week
**sentier** ⓜ son·tyay footpath
**service** ⓜ sair·vees service • service charge
**serviette** ⓕ sair·vyet briefcase • napkin • towel
**sœur** ⓕ ser sister
**soie** ⓕ swa silk
**soir** ⓜ swar evening
**soirée** ⓕ swa·ray night out • party
**sortie** ⓕ sor·tee exit
**sortir** sor·teer go out
**sous-titres** ⓜ soo·tee·trer subtitles
**sous-vêtements** ⓜ soo·vet·mon underwear
**soutien-gorge** ⓜ soo·tyung·gorzh bra
**sparadrap** ⓜ spa·ra·dra Band-Aid
**spectacle** ⓜ spek·ta·kler performance • show

**station** ① **de métro** sta·syon der may·tro metro station

**station** ① **de taxi** sta·syon der tak·see taxi stand

**station-service** ① sta·syon·sair·vees petrol station

**sud** ⓜ sewd south

**supérette** ① **de quartier** sew·pay·ret der kar·tyay convenience store

**supermarché** ⓜ sew·pair·mar·shay supermarket

## - t -

**tableau** ⓜ ta·blo painting (a work)

**taie** ① **d'oreiller** tay do·ray·yay pillowcase

**taille** ① tai size (general)

**tailleur** ⓜ ta·yer tailor

**tante** ① tont aunt

**tarif** ⓜ ta·reef fare

**taux** ⓜ **de change** to der shonzh currency exchange

**taxe** ① **d'aéroport** taks da·ay·ro·por airport tax

**télécarte** ① tay·lay·kart phone card

**téléphone** ⓜ **portable** tay·lay·fon por·ta·bler mobile phone

**télésiège** ⓜ tay·lay·syezh chairlift (skiing)

**timbre** ⓜ tum·brer stamp

**tôt** to early

**tout(e)** ⓜ/① too(t) everything

**toux** ① too cough

**traiteur** ⓜ tre·ter delicatessen

## - v -

**vacances** ① pl va·kons holidays • vacation

**valider** va·lee·day validate

**valise** ① va·leez suitcase

**vélo** ⓜ vay·lo bicycle

**vert(e)** ⓜ/① vair(t) green

**veste** ① vest jacket

**vestiaire** ⓜ vays·tyair cloakroom

**vêtements** ⓜ vet·mon clothing

**viande** ① vyond meat

**ville** ① veel city • town

**vin** ⓜ vun wine

**visite** ① **guidée** vee·zeet gee·day guided tour

**voie de terre** vw der tair surface mail (land)

**voie maritime** vwa ma·ree·teem surface mail (sea)

**voiture** ① vwa·tewr car

**vol** ⓜ vol flight • robbery

**volé(e)** ⓜ/① vo·lay stolen

**voyage** ⓜ vwa·yazh journey • tour • trip

**— d'affaires** da·fair business trip

**voyageur/voyageuse** ⓜ/① vwa·ya·zher/vwa·ya·zherz passenger

**vue** ① vew view

## - w -

**wagon-lit** ⓜ va·gon·lee sleeping car

**wagon-restaurant** ⓜ va·gon·res·to·ron dining car

**Acknowledgments**
**Associate Product Director** Angela Tinson
**Production Editors** Clare Healy, Kathryn Rowan
**Language Writers** Michael Janes, Jean-Pierre Masclef, Jean-Bernard Carillet
**Cover Researcher** Gwen Cotter
**Book Designer** Ania Lenihan

**Thanks**
Kate Chapman, James Hardy, Indra Kilfoyle, Wibowo Rusli, Juan Winata

**Published by Lonely Planet Global Ltd**
CRN 554153

5th Edition – August 2023
Text © Lonely Planet 2023
**Cover Image** Promenade des Anglais, Nice, Kevincho.Photography/
Shutterstock ©

Printed in China  10 9 8 7 6 5 4 3 2 1

**Contact** lonelyplanet.com/contact

Although the authors and Lonely Planet try to make the information as accurate as possible, we accept no responsibility for any loss, injury or inconvenience sustained by anyone using this book.

Paper in this book is certified against the Forest Stewardship Council™ standards. FSC™ promotes environmentally responsible, socially beneficial and economically viable management of the world's forests.

# Index

# 10. Phrases to Get You Talking

| | |
|---|---|
| **Hello.** | Bonjour.<br>bon·zhoor |
| **Goodbye.** | Au revoir.<br>o rer·vwar |
| **Please.** | S'il vous plaît.<br>seel voo play |
| **Thank you.** | Merci.<br>mair·see |
| **Excuse me.** | Excusez-moi.<br>ek·skew·zay·mwa |
| **Sorry.** | Pardon.<br>par·don |
| **Yes.** | Oui.<br>wee |
| **No.** | Non.<br>non |
| **I don't understand.** | Je ne comprends pas.<br>zher ner kom·pron pa |
| **How much is it?** | C'est combien?<br>say kom·byun |